DAVID
and
GOLIATH

HOW INDEPENDENT RETAILERS
CAN TAKE ON THE GIANTS AND WIN

DAVID
and
GOLIATH

HOW INDEPENDENT RETAILERS
CAN TAKE ON THE GIANTS AND WIN

IAN RETALLICK

RETHINK PRESS

First published in Great Britain 2017
by Rethink Press (www.rethinkpress.com)

Cover image © depositphotos / biblebox

PRAISE

'A must read for all independent retailers. Ian concisely shows the real issues facing retailers and gives credible and simple-to-follow ways in which to stay ahead of the game. Even as a successful retailer, the insights contained in Ian's book help to re-enforce all the things you are doing right so you know where to focus. A brilliant book that can help independent retailers to better predict the future of retail and how to make sure you rise above the game.'

Yuvi Rana
Director, Yuvilite Ltd

'I'm so glad to have read Ian's book. It is difficult to know how to move forward with this constant battle of the price wars and price matching demands. I have taken away some very good ideas and reminded myself that we do have a lot to offer our customers who are prepared to value us and our showroom. I struggle greatly with singing our praises using social media and asking others to do the same, but I can see there would be huge benefits from doing this. I will re-read this in greater detail and I will recommend other members of staff do the same. In short – in a very difficult time for small retailers this has been an inspiring and motivating read. I have taken away some great ideas and will be singing my praises to all who will listen!'

Julie Gwilliam
Director, The Famous Little Lamp Shop

'A true inspiration! The turn to guide for the independent retailer in a world of giants. This book has made me look at myself as an independent retailer and my business from a different angle. Rather than bemoan the giant retailers, it is time to take them head on and embrace the changes and challenges and differentiate ourselves. I found Ian's book informative motivational and a very pleasant read.'

Andy Lobb
Managing Partner, The Lampshade Warehouse Lighting Outlet

David and Goliath took us on an insightful, thought-provoking journey which encompassed just the right amount of personal story telling, historical references and meaningful examples. Describing the book as an "easy read" is by no means meant as a negative, in fact quite the opposite. The book flows with ease through its concepts, allowing the reader to concentrate on the useful content rather than be distracted by overdone analogies or a condescending tone (neither of which are present!). We also appreciated the concise summaries at the end of each chapter as they didn't labour the point. Overall, the book is beautifully written and at points effortlessly brings the reader back to the title characters/story of *David and Goliath*. We enjoyed the read and there is no doubt in our minds that as an independent retailer we will benefit from the resulting thought process and from implementing the lessons.'

Libby Crew, Paul Bullingham
Proprietor, Fusion Lighting, Dorchester

CONTENTS

Introduction	**3**
The Power Of Why	**11**
What do you really want?	16
How much are you worth?	18
Learning from history	20
Stone One – Who Is Your Ideal Customer?	**25**
The giraffe and the elephant	25
Who is your ideal customer?	28
Create a customer profile	35
What business are you really in?	39
Describe your ideal customer	44
Stone One summary	48
Stone Two – How To Create A Compelling Message	**49**
The power of words	50
Messages that turn customers off	56
Three steps to creating the right message	57
Share, review, revise and polish	66
Stone Two summary	70
Stone Three – The Product Ecosystem	**71**
What is the product ecosystem?	72
Stepping stones to your core products	83
What customers will pay	87

Finding the right suppliers 93

Stone Three summary 99

Stone Four – The Power Of Prospecting **101**

Flecks of gold 102

Marginal gains 108

Overcoming your prospecting Goliaths 110

Speaking engagements 120

Proactive prospecting 122

Stone Four summary 124

Stone Five – You Are The Brand **125**

A dash of personality 129

Social media and personal branding 137

Content is key 145

When and how to sell on social media 147

Measuring results 148

Stone Five summary 150

Conclusion **153**

Acknowledgements **158**

About The Author **160**

FOREWORD

Reading Ian's book has been interesting because in addition to teaching me some new skills it has also reminded me of a number of other business truths that had slipped from the forefront of my mind.

Notwithstanding they are much bigger businesses than PAGAZZI, we have demonstrated that it is possible to compete with the giants through specialisation – and this book will provide you with the key building blocks for doing the same.

It is also worth noting that you don't need to be an 'expert' in something before becoming a specialist retailer. I knew nothing about lighting in 1980, but learned quickly.

While it is true that modern retailing is to a certain extent more complex, requiring modern thinking and skill sets, it also levels the playing field for good specialist retailers and if implemented correctly, can provide an environment that allows them to compete with the retail giants. Ian's Five Stones will provide you with a framework for doing so.

Regardless of whether you are starting out in retail for the first time, or are looking for a way to change the direction of an existing business, there are key messages and actions in the book that will be of great use to you.

Laura Pagan is the Founder and Managing Director of PAGAZZI. The company, which started trading in 1980, operates eighteen stores and is now the largest specialist Lighting and Mirror retailer in the U.K.

INTRODUCTION

My dad was in retail his whole life. He worked for large retail chains in the UK and South Africa and was well known for taking failing stores and turning them into successful and thriving outlets. I remember visiting him at work and later working with him, observing his gift for getting the best out of his staff.

He was a hard worker and, even though I was half his age, I struggled to keep pace with him. He was patient and caring and had a knack of melting the hearts of even the most difficult customers.

However, when he decided to start his own business, he struggled to make money. In fact, he tried three different businesses and struggled every time. What happened? He was the same person with the same skills and experience, and yet he was unable to run a profitable business on his own.

I don't believe he was the only retailer to face these challenges. I know many smart independent retailers who are so busy with the day to day demands of their business that they often miss golden nuggets of opportunity sitting on their doorstep.

My dad died suddenly many years ago, before he could experience success as an independent retailer. It's been nearly thirty years since his death, and since then I have learned many new and exciting things about retail, business and sales. Even though I will never be able to share these with my dad, I am grateful for the privilege of being able to share them with you.

I believe wholeheartedly in the independent retailer. There is a long life ahead for bricks-and-mortar retailers if we are prepared to specialise. By implementing the principles taught in this book, you can become a specialist retailer and enjoy a thriving and profitable business. My purpose – my 'why' in writing this book – is to make a difference in your business. Please allow me to join you on your journey.

When David confronted Goliath, he took five smooth stones in preparation for the fight. Against impossible odds, he took on this giant and slew him with the first stone. In *David and Goliath, How Independent Retailers Can Take On The Giants And Win*, you will be given five stones (five steps) to help you slay the giants in your industry so that you can transform your business from an independent to a specialist retailer. When you specialise, you immediately separate yourself from your competitors. As a result, you attract more of the right kind of customers, which leads to increased sales.

I have been in sales for over forty years, and like my dad I have had my fair share of disappointments. At school I remember being labelled thick and stupid – and that was just from the teachers! In my first twenty years of business, I had twelve jobs and four business failures. Some would say that I wasn't very smart or capable of holding down a job. In many ways, they would be right.

However, I believe that life is a great teacher. After having so many setbacks, I began to recognise some flaws in my personality that were the cause of my failures. There are too many to share them all in this book, and I do have an ego to protect, but I will share a few of them in the hope that they will benefit you and your business.

The first and most obvious flaw was that I lacked sustained persistence. We can all be persistent, but it's only when we are prepared to persist over long periods of time and push through the storms of life that we will see the light of day.

I also lacked real faith and vision. I used to set grand and lofty goals and I thought I had the faith to succeed, but really, I did not. It was all just a dream.

Real faith and vision go hand in hand. In the Bible, Proverbs 29:18 tells us *'Where there is no vision, the people perish'*. Imagine that. What if we applied this to our industry – *'Where there is no vision, the independent retailers perish'*? How does that sound?

It is important to have a clear and realistic vision for your business. When you have a clear vision of what you want to achieve, you are better equipped to overcome the challenges you will inevitably face in running a thriving business.

The antithesis of faith is fear. Much of my motivation was grounded by fear, which is a negative and destructive emotion. As I learned to transform my fears into faith, I acted from a place of confidence and realism that helped me to achieve financial success.

Armed with sustained persistence, faith and vision, I started my fifth business in 2007 supplying decorative lighting to independent retailers and department stores. I'm pleased to say that business is good and going from strength to strength. The same five steps – the stones – that helped me can also help you to achieve sustained success and a lifestyle that matches your dreams.

Independent retailers are facing their toughest challenge since the rise of the chain stores in the 1930s. Today, big online retailers and national chains have an insatiable need to gobble up market share on an unprecedented level. Most independent retailers are hardworking and know their trade, but they simply can't compete with these giants and their massive financial muscle.

On top of this, the playing field is uneven because more and more customers are using bricks-and-mortar retailers as a convenient showroom to view products they have seen online. They seek advice and expertise from the sales staff, and then buy the exact same product online for a fraction of the cost.

With higher overheads and fewer resources, how can you compete, thrive and build a prosperous retail business? I have visited hundreds of independent retailers and I can tell in minutes when I am in a specialist store. Specialist retailers don't pander to the masses; they carefully select stock that will appeal to their ideal customer. They are able to give remarkable service because they aren't trying to be all things to all people.

Stone One will help you to identify your target customer by creating a detailed customer profile. In Stone Two, you will learn how to create a powerful and compelling message that will resonate with your ideal customer. We then explore the product ecosystem in Stone Three, creating a range of core products that will appeal to your target market. In Stone Four, we will discuss how to attract your ideal customer by harnessing the power of prospecting. With Stones One to Four in place, you will then be ready to implement Stone Five which will help you to increase market share by raising your personal profile.

In sales there is no such thing as B2B or even B2C. Only P2P – people to people. And people buy from people. Stone Five is a vital ingredient, and yet it is the least understood by most independent retailers. By allowing your personality to shine through, you create a real connection with your customer, which leads to a loyal following of ideal customers.

Let's get started by examining the power of why.

THE POWER OF WHY

Before you proceed to learn the principles in this book, you may want to take a moment to consider why you are in business. The reason that David was able to defeat Goliath was because he had a big enough reason to fight in the first place – his 'why'.

David was a young shepherd and of no great significance when Israel faced the Philistines in battle. For forty days, Goliath, a nine-foot giant, taunted the Israeli army to send out their best soldier to fight him. He proclaimed that if he lost the fight, the Philistines would become servants to the Israelites, but if he won, Israel would become servants to the Philistines.

When David delivered supplies to the men of Israel, he was surprised to see them recoiling with fear and fleeing from Goliath. David told Saul, the King of Israel, that he would fight Goliath, but Saul said he was too young and Goliath was a highly trained soldier. David explained that with God's help, he had successfully defended his father's sheep from a lion and a bear, and God would also help him slay Goliath.

Saul finally agreed to allow David to fight Goliath, but insisted on protecting him with a full suit of armour, a heavy shield and a large sword. David was weighed down and said that he couldn't fight in the heavy armour. Instead, he went into battle with five smooth stones and a sling.

David's older brothers were perhaps a little embarrassed that they had not already gone to battle Goliath, so they told David he was being mischievous and had only really come to watch the battle. David's reply was humble and yet profound.

'Is there not a cause?'

He reminded them of why they were fighting in the first place. This wasn't just a battle of two armies, it was a fight for freedom and liberty. With unshakable faith and conviction, he went into battle with Goliath, fighting on his own terms and in his own way[1].

When you take on the giants in your industry, you will need to have a deep rooted 'why'. Knowing your why is incredibly powerful. It can help you through even the toughest situations. Great leaders such as Bill Gates, James Dyson and Richard Branson all know why they are in business, and that is how they are able to push through their darkest moments with patience and determination until they succeed.

Orville and Wilbur Wright invented the flying machine. After hundreds of experiments and countless failures, Wilbur Wright became discouraged and exclaimed, 'Not within a thousand years will man ever fly[2]!'

However, his good friend Octave Chanute urged him and his brother not to give up, arguing that if they did, 'It would be a long time before anyone else would come as near to understanding the problem or how to work towards a solution'[3].

In essence, Chanute reminded the Wright brothers of their why.

Your why is not something you can create or invent. It is something that is already there, but you will need to discover it if you want to specialise and take on the giants.

So how do you discover your why? How do you find your inner conviction? This is not easy because your why is not measurable. You cannot set a date to achieve it, nor can you attach a monetary figure to it.

For years, I thought that you discovered your why by looking to the future. For goals, targets, achievements and milestones, that may be true. But as Simon Sinek explains in his book *Start With Why*, you discover your why by looking to your past[4].

When I heard this, I was literally blown away – if you want to discover your why, you need to search your past.

When I began searching for my why, I needed time and deep reflection. The answer didn't come all at once; instead, it was like the early morning dew on the grass. A drop falls here and a drop there. Over time, thoughts and ideas came to me, and like a jigsaw puzzle, my why became clear.

When you understand why you are in business, you are no longer just working to make money. Instead, you are marching towards a cause greater than yourself. As you implement the ideas in this book, you will need to make a series of minor changes that may seem uncomfortable at first, but over time will make a big difference in your business. When these changes are connected and underscored by your why, your results accelerate exponentially.

In the early 1980s, Nick Faldo was recognised as a top-class golf professional, but he had not yet won a major tournament. In 1985, he recruited David Leadbetter, a professional coach, to help him change his game so that he could reach his potential on the world tour.

David told him that he would have to change every aspect of his game and that it would probably take up to two years before he saw any significant improvements. During that time, he worked on getting Nick's posture right, refining his swing and changing his grip. David helped him change his stance and the way he rotated his body, and many other minor but crucial things.

While he was implementing the changes, Nick's game slumped to such a low that the media began to criticise him and his coach. But Nick knew that with patience and persistence, he would perfect his game.

Nick Faldo eventually won six major tournaments and held the number one spot for 97 weeks.

WHAT DO YOU REALLY WANT?

Once you understand why you are doing what you are doing, you need to decide what it is you want. Imagine what your life would look like if you already had financial freedom. How would you feel? What would you do differently? What fun things would you do that you can't afford now? What significant purchases would you make? Where would you go on holiday? How often?

What would you like to learn? What hobbies would you like to take up? Which sporting achievements would you like to attain? What contributions would you like to make? What investments? What would you like to see happen in your family life?

Now write down when you would like to achieve these goals. Be realistic. I suggest you set your goal no more than three to five years ahead. If your goal is too far in the future, your mind won't sense any urgency and is less likely to come up with solutions to help you achieve it. When you know what you want to achieve and when you want to achieve it by, you are in a better position to make plans.

Last year, I decided to climb Ben Nevis, the UK's highest mountain. I was in my mid-fifties and unfit. I knew that if I attempted to climb Ben Nevis in my physical state at the time, I would fail.

The first thing I did was to research the time it would take to get to the top. What kind of food and hydration would I need? What clothing and equipment would I need, and what would I do if anything went wrong? I then set a date to make the climb and enlisted the help of my son and son-in-law. If I struggled or fell, they could carry me to the top and back down again, so at least I would have some measure of success.

For six months prior to our climb, I walked three times a week. At first I did gentle walks by the river, and then I progressed to regular hill walking where I built stamina and mental strength. I became more and more confident in my ability and knew that I was ready to climb the highest mountain in the UK.

I am pleased to say that we climbed Ben Nevis on a beautiful, clear day and saw some spectacular views. I felt exhilarated when we made it to the top, where we had great fun throwing snowballs at each other.

The principles I learned in climbing Ben Nevis can be applied to your business. Know what you want – only you can decide what this is. Set a date and make a plan to achieve it. The five stones outlined in this book will help you to climb to the summit of your mountain. I hope you have fun.

HOW MUCH ARE YOU WORTH?

Now would be a great time to calculate what you are worth. Do you know? Most people don't, and so they don't know how much it's costing them when they waste time on low value activities.

You need to know what your daily rate is so that you can know your value. The best way to do this is to write down your annual income, divide it by twelve, and then divide that figure by twenty-four (based on a six-day working week).

Now decide how much you want to earn every day. Do you want to double your income, or perhaps even triple it? If you want to triple your income, what will your daily worth be when you achieve this goal?

Once you know what your new daily rate will be, write it down in a prominent place where you will see it every day. Better still, put that amount of cash in your pocket so you can see and feel it.

Your time is valuable, so you need to ensure that you are being paid what you are worth. It's only when you place the right value on your time that you are able to spend time on the things that are most worthy. Then you will see opportunities that will help you to achieve your new daily rate.

LEARNING FROM HISTORY

Frank Woolworth launched his variety stores known as 'Five-and-Dimes' in 1879 in Lancaster, Pennsylvania, but it was only in the early 20th century that chain stores reached gigantic proportions and became a real threat to independent retailers in America and the UK. The rhetoric of the day was that national chain stores could provide low-priced goods for the masses because of their ability to buy in bulk. Newspapers and trade journals propagated the idea that large chain stores were efficient, and that small independent retailers were inefficient and ripping customers off by charging higher prices.

Lord Beaverbrook raised the warning voice in an article written for the *Daily Express* in 1930.

Rather more than two centuries ago, Louis XIV called us a nation of shopkeepers. To-day I am afraid, he would call us a nation of inefficient shopkeepers. It is not enough for us to follow the tradition of his days; we must strike out on the new lines to meet the utterly changed conditions of modern city life[5].

These fears were typical of the time, and they reflected the belief that a section of the trade had failed to keep pace with a changing economic and social climate.

Lord Beaverbrook's warning is as relevant now as it was then. His call in the 1930s was for small shopkeepers to break away from the traditions of their past and to meet the changing conditions of the time. There were many small shopkeepers who went to the wall in the 1930s because they were unable or unwilling to adapt to the changing climate. But those who improved efficiencies and smartened up their stores became strong and profitable.

It is my belief that independent retailers today need to meet the changing conditions of our time by becoming specialist retailers. The giant online retailers and national chain stores have a firm grip on the market, and independent retailers who cling to the traditions of the past will at best limp along, struggling to make a living.

Having great staff, excellent customer service and a smart showroom with tight controls on stock and bookkeeping is just a starting point. Even the most loyal customers are easily persuaded to buy from the giants if the price and quality are right. Today you need to outsmart and outthink the giants, just as David outsmarted Goliath by playing to his strengths.

National chain stores and online retailers offer a great service and they can be great places to shop. As an independent, your focus needs to be to offer something unique that is not found in the big stores. I appreciate that this is not easy, but with ingenuity, creativity and hard work, you can make a difference and succeed.

In June 1935, the *Small Trader* began a series called 'How To Start Out In Business', with reference to a range of trades in which small-scale shopkeepers could be found in large numbers. The articles suggested ways to improve efficiencies and compete with the larger chains. Alluding to the story of David slaying Goliath with a stone, one writer argued that *'When David is an independent trader, and Goliath a chain store, you must bring your weapons up to date*[6]*.'*

Do you need to bring your weapons up to date? Are you fighting for the same customer with the same products and the same message as the giants?

History is a great teacher. Just as independent retailers survived the rise of the national chains in the 1930s, you can take on the giants in your industry and win. I am not anti-chain store – while I might not agree with all of their practices, I believe there is a place for them as well as the independent retailer. By differentiating yourself from the giants and offering that personal touch, you can survive the storms. Many independent retailers from the early 20th century are still trading today, such as Evans Cycles and the Atlantis Bookshop, both based in London. Reidys Home of Music is still a family run business, established in 1922 in Blackburn, Lancashire.

The principles taught in this book are not designed to take away from your expertise, but to add to it. It will take effort to try new things, and like David slaying Goliath, you will need a large dose of courage. It is a privilege for me to walk with you on your journey and share a few ideas that I hope will reinvigorate your passion for your business. Please keep in touch. I would love to hear about your successes, and it's OK if you want to tell me about the tough times as well.

1. 1 Samuel 17, King James Version of the Bible.

2 and 3. Fred C. Kelly, *The Wright Brothers*. Pickle Partners Publishing, Kindle Edition 2016, location 831. Original text published in 1943 under the same title.

4. Simon Sinek, *Start with Why*. London: Portfolio Penguin, 2011, page 214.

5. *Daily Express,* 17 Jan 1930. Cited by Simon Phillips and Andrew Alexander, Enterprise and Society, 2005, Cambridge University Press.

6. *Independent Trader and Retailers Review* 1 (12), June 1936: 375–76. Cited by Simon Phillips and Andrew Alexander, Enterprise and Society, 2005, Cambridge University Press.

WHO IS YOUR IDEAL CUSTOMER?

THE GIRAFFE AND THE ELEPHANT

One day a giraffe decided to open a store selling clothing. He built a wonderful showroom with tall ceilings and narrow doors so that his giraffe customers could easily visit and buy his goods. He built shelving high on the walls so that his customers could try on the wonderful array of hats. The fitting rooms had tall and thin mirrors for his customers to see how good they looked. He then created a website and a social media profile aimed at attracting more customers into his showroom.

A few weeks after opening, he met his good friend the elephant and invited him to his store. But when the elephant tried to enter the store, he was too wide to fit through the narrow doors. The giraffe saw his dilemma and rushed to his aid.

'Come around the back and we'll let you in through the back entrance. Those doors have been made bigger for our deliveries.'

The elephant was relieved and pleased to enter the giraffe's store to see the new clothes. He was delighted with the colourful range, but when he tried them on, they were too tight. He liked the look of the hats, but they were just out of his reach.

The giraffe was embarrassed and disappointed that nothing was suitable for the elephant. The elephant left the store feeling dejected and down in the trunk.

With the best of intentions, the giraffe could not help the elephant. He had correctly identified his ideal customer and stocked a fashionable range of clothing for his giraffe friends, but the style and size would never suit the elephant. He was clearly not the giraffe's target market.

And that's OK. The purpose of this book is to help independent retailers to become specialist retailers. A specialist by nature has a narrow field of expertise. When you are a specialist, you are in a position to charge a premium price for your products and services because customers want what you have to offer. You know who your target customer is and you focus your efforts in satisfying and exceeding their needs.

Identifying your ideal customer may not be as easy as it was for the giraffe, but the principles are the same. Creating a customer profile that is clear and specific is the first step in attracting more of the right kind of customers to your business. When you have a well-defined customer profile, you are in an ideal position to provide great products and services that will immediately separate you from the giants in your industry.

I recently bought a suit from a local independent retailer who specialises in high end men's clothing. If I had asked for a cheap suit, he would have politely shown me the door. Likewise, if I went to McDonald's and ordered a medium-rare sirloin steak, the staff would most likely direct me to my nearest steakhouse. Knowing your target customer is not always about price.

WHO IS YOUR IDEAL CUSTOMER?

I have asked many retailers this question, but the answer they usually give is not who their ideal customer is, but who their customer is at the moment. This is understandable. It is easy to confuse your regular customers with your ideal customer. But they are not necessarily the same.

When I ask the same retailers if they ever get customers who are happy with their service and willingly buy their core products, they usually say yes. I recently suggested to a retailer whom I have known for many years that all he needs to do is to get more of that kind of customer. He smiled in disbelief and told me that there weren't any more to be found. Although I agree that it is not easy to get more ideal customers, it is possible.

We will discuss how and where to find more of your target market in Stone Four – The Power Of Prospecting.

Running an independent retail business can be overwhelming. As a business owner, you often have many hats to wear, and your responsibilities can range from sales and marketing to accountancy, to managing and motivating staff. Some days you can spend hours with Mr and Mrs Difficult who can stretch your patience to the limit and beyond. While you're doing your best to serve them, other customers are asking you to price match a product they found on Google. It is likely you rarely have time to take a step back and consider the opportunities that are often sitting right on your doorstep.

And then you get that special day when Mr and Mrs Ideal come in and they are just wonderful. They love you and they love your products. They listen to your advice and are happy to buy from you based on your recommendations, and they don't even ask for a discount. You feel elated, there is a skip in your step and your enthusiasm is contagious. If only you could get more of this kind of customer, your business would be thriving and you would be a lot happier.

It begins with identifying in specific detail who your ideal customer is. Why do you need to be specific? Because the clearer you are, the more likely it is you will get what you are looking for.

When your thinking is crystallised, your mind is better equipped to put plans into place to attract more of your ideal customer. But if you have a vague and hazy picture, you will get vague and hazy results. When you know precisely what kind of customer you want to attract, stock more of the kind of products that they will want to buy, designed with them in mind. Aim your marketing and social media campaigns specifically at them, creating a compelling message around their needs and desires. When you prospect for new business, you will be prospecting for your ideal customer, and when you promote your personal brand, you will share your expertise and insights in a way that will appeal to them.

It is only when you have a clear understanding of your target customer that you can implement the other four stones in the book.

Before we create a customer profile, let's consider your ideal customer and what is really important to them. When David took on Goliath, he knew what was important. He had made covenants with God and he was not prepared to compromise his values for anything. There will be some generic things that are important to all customers and there will be things that are more specific to your ideal customer. Let's begin with the general things that are uppermost in people's minds when they are seeking products and services.

In 1943, Abraham Maslow developed a theory of motivation which became known as Maslow's Hierarchy of Needs. He based his study on exemplary achievers such as Albert Einstein, Jane Addams, Eleanor Roosevelt and Frederick Douglass. He also studied the healthiest 1% of the college student population in America, concluding that there is a Hierarchy of Needs in all of us.

It starts with our basic need for nourishment and shelter, and then our need for security and safety. As these needs are satisfied, we develop a desire to belong and feel accepted. Over time, our need to be recognised and respected grows, as does our desire to be self-actualised.

When you are self-actualised, you are motivated to realise your full potential. It is a place where you unlock your creativity, seek spiritual truths and pursue knowledge. It is also a place where you can enjoy peak experiences. A peak experience is when everything flows perfectly and you feel that you are in the zone.

They are moments of ecstasy which cannot be bought, cannot be guaranteed, cannot even be sought...but one can set up the conditions so that peak experiences are more likely.

Abraham Maslow

MASLOW'S HIERARCHY OF NEEDS[1]

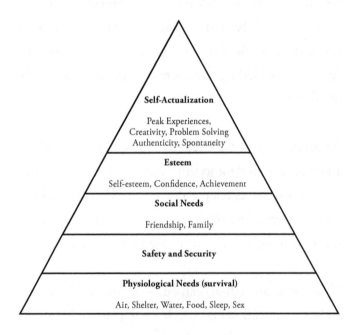

Self-Actualization

Peak Experiences,
Creativity, Problem Solving
Authenticity, Spontaneity

Esteem

Self-esteem, Confidence, Achievement

Social Needs

Friendship, Family

Safety and Security

Physiological Needs (survival)

Air, Shelter, Water, Food, Sleep, Sex

The products or services you sell may appeal to some or all of your customers' needs, according to Maslow's Hierarchy. Do all you can to lift your customer to the top of the hierarchy by creating an environment where they are most likely to enjoy peak experiences. Peak experiences are not easy to capture, but you can create the circumstances that will increase the chances for your customers to enjoy them.

Last year, my wife and I enjoyed a red-letter day at The Battle Proms in the glorious grounds of Blenheim Palace in Oxfordshire. We arrived early because we wanted to find a nice spot to lay out our picnic and chairs. We felt invigorated, relaxed and at peace all at the same time. I remember telling my wife that it all felt surreal and calming being able to take our time. There's a chance the organisers weren't thinking of Maslow's Hierarchy when they initiated this event, but unwittingly they had created an environment where we could enjoy the moment as if time had stood still.

How can you create moments of peak experiences for your customers? Think about times when you have enjoyed such moments. How did you feel? How can you help your customers feel the same way?

We are fortunate to live in a country where most of our customers' basic needs for nourishment and shelter are satisfied, but they will have a need to feel safe and secure. The more you can reassure your customer that they can trust you and that they are safe buying from you, the more likely they will be to do business with your company.

Moving up the hierarchy, customers like to belong and feel accepted. How does this translate to selling your products? If your ideal customer is a risk-taker, they are less likely to worry about the approval of their friends. But if they are more cautious, they won't want to risk the disapproval of their friends and family by purchasing anything outlandish or obscure.

If you are selling luxury or premium products, you will most likely be appealing to your customers' need for recognition, respect and status. Someone who is buying a tailored suit from Savile Row is not primarily interested in keeping warm. They are seeking the prestige that comes from wearing an exclusive suit that sets them apart and makes them feel and look amazing.

The need for recognition and status is a powerful motivator, and if you can appeal to this emotion you will be pleasantly surprised by the increased turnover. However, you need to be subtle because most customers will go to great lengths to deny that this is their true motivation. What is it about your products and services that will appeal to your customers' need to feel respected and important?

CREATE A CUSTOMER PROFILE

A customer profile is a representation of the kind of customer who is either buying from you now or whom you would like to buy from you. There may be more than one customer profile that you would like to attract, but it's important to define who your ideal customers are so that you target the right ones.

For each customer profile, gather as much information as possible. The more accurate your information, the better you will be able to target the customers, which is vital when you begin prospecting for new business.

The simplest way to generate a customer profile for a retailer is to gather demographic information from a loyalty programme. If your customers' purchases are logged, you can also identify different types of customer for different types of product. When you record the time of day and the day of the week your customer has made a purchase, profiling becomes even more interesting and detailed.

If you don't run a loyalty programme, then collect the postcodes of shoppers over a week, together with the time of day and the day of the week they visited, and draft a profile from that list.

When you ask questions about your ideal customer, remove yourself from your products and services. Put yourself in your customers' shoes and consider what problems they have. What keeps them awake at night?

I recently travelled back from an exhibition in Germany with two customers. Laura and Rebecca own a large and busy family business in Scotland and the north of England. I was interested to hear their views so I asked them a bunch of questions about their business, careful not to ask them anything about my products and service. I wanted to know about their problems and what was important to them, irrespective of my business. Our journey to the airport took about an hour, and in that time I was grateful for their candid and honest responses.

When you use this approach, you will uncover the real issues and frustrations customers face, rather than what sounds immediately relevant to your business. The quality of the answers you get is determined by the quality of the questions you ask. It is a good idea to avoid asking frivolous questions. I had my questions prepared on a small card and so it was easy to stay on track. I also asked Laura and Rebecca permission to record their answers and promised to keep any sensitive material confidential.

By the time we got to the airport, we were able to uncover that their two main challenges were lack of time and staff management. I was not in a position to address their staffing challenges, but I was able to help them with their time problems.

How could my decorative lighting help them save time? My lights couldn't help, but what about how I delivered them? What if we delivered products directly to Laura and Rebecca's customers to save their staff from spending time repackaging and redirecting orders? What if we saved them time by installing new display stands complete with fittings?

A great place to start building your customer profile is by speaking to your existing customers. Here are a few questions you could ask to help create your ideal customer profile:

- Where do they like to shop?
- Do they like the movies or do they prefer the theatre?
- What sports and hobbies do they love?
- What is important to them when they buy products?
- What frustrates them about shopping?
- Why do they buy from certain kinds of shops?
- What problems do they have that your products can solve?
- Why should your ideal customer buy from you rather than someone else?
- Which area or town do they live in?
- How often do they buy your kind of product?
- What are their goals and aspirations?
- What is their age, education, occupation or business?
- Where is your ideal customer most likely to buy your products?

These types of questions will help you to create a picture of your ideal customer. The more questions you can answer about your customers, the closer you will get to defining your ideal customer.

WHAT BUSINESS ARE YOU REALLY IN?

There is an inseparable link between what business you are in and who your ideal customer is. At first this may sound like an obvious statement. But it is worth making every effort to gain a clear understanding of what business you are *really* in.

When I ask this question, most retailers will reply in relation to their products – 'I am in the lighting business' or 'I sell furniture'; 'I sell shoes' or 'I run a clothing store'. While these statements may be true, they are far too narrow and set you up to be just like all the other retailers who also sell what you sell. This makes it difficult for your customer to differentiate you from your competitors, which means they will struggle to find reasons to buy from you.

Theodore Levitt is well known for his essays on marketing myopia where he explains the downfall of large industries which defined their businesses too narrowly. He explains that the railways didn't stop growing because the need for passenger and freight transportation declined. They stopped growing because this need was filled by other industries such as cars, lorries and aeroplanes. The railway industry in the early 1900s focused on its product rather than its customer. When the aviation industry developed passenger travel by air, and affordable and comfortable coaches could carry customers over long distances, the railway owners did not see them as competitors. They continued to define themselves as rail travel providers, which resulted in a dramatic loss of sales with many of them going out of business, when actually they were in the transportation business.

This is a classic mistake made by the majority of businesses, large and small. Levitt suggests that businesses will do better if they concentrate on meeting customers' needs rather than selling products[2].

Someone selling sofas may see themselves as a furniture retailer, but what business are they really in? A few years ago, we bought a new leather lounge suite. My wife and I did our research and decided we wanted a sofa that looked great and felt comfortable. I particularly wanted a version with soft, low arms so I could stretch out and lie on it while watching TV (that's if I got there before my children).

Since buying our perfect sofa, we have built many wonderful memories of family and friends gathered together on it to enjoy hours of fun and games. So instead of just selling sofas, could a furniture retailer be selling memories?

In 2012, the furniture store DFS changed its price led advertising campaigns to emotion-led advertising. The ads showed children playing on a sofa, the tag line being 'Making every day more comfortable' with a heart shaped logo. Appealing to our emotions has a more lasting effect than selling on price[3].

John Lewis is well known for Christmas commercials that tug at our heartstrings. In 2015, it launched the man on the moon commercial. An old man was seen all alone on the moon by a young girl through her telescope. She felt sorry for him and so she attached one of her Christmas presents to some balloons and sent it to the man on the moon. The message highlighted the plight of thousands of individuals who are alone at Christmas time, and the emotional connection was that the kind of people who buy from John Lewis are kind and considerate to lonely people. Even if that isn't true, the advert created a feel-good factor that drew customers to buy John Lewis products.

The retailer Dreams doesn't sell beds, it sells a good night's sleep, 'Because sleep matters'. Dreams recently launched an advertising campaign to alert the nation to replace their mattress every eight years. If you're like me, you probably don't remember how long you've had your mattress, so Dreams now puts a date on each of its mattresses so you know when to replace it. Dreams makes excellent mattresses, but so do many other manufacturers. This one just identified two areas that were important to its customers and focused its marketing campaign on those.

Ikea doesn't believe in perfect homes. The brand believes in homes that are a perfect reflection of the people who live in them. Ikea creates furniture and displays it in different room sets that look appealing and inviting and affordable. The advertising people at Ikea understood early on that they weren't just selling furniture, they were selling concepts and ideas that would inspire their ideal customer to see possibilities they had never imagined.

What is the emotional appeal of your brand or company? How can you replace an emphasis on price with an emotionally led campaign? More importantly, how can you make it real and sincere? How can you prompt your customers to think differently about themselves, your products and you as a company?

It is worth every effort to consider what business you are really in. You may want to have a brainstorming session with your staff or a trusted friend. Place yourself in your customers' shoes, or lounge, or wherever your products are found, and see your business from their point of view.

You could even ask a few customers how they feel about your business or industry. Listen to their feelings and emotions. What excites them about your products or services? How can you help them to think differently about you and your business?

By redefining your business, you see yourself in a different light. With a change of focus from products to customer, you are able to separate yourself from the crowd. Over time, you will be seen as the expert in your field and your customers will buy from you because they sense that you genuinely care about them.

As you gain a clearer understanding of what business you are in, you will be better equipped to define who your target customer really is.

DESCRIBE YOUR IDEAL CUSTOMER

Once you've gathered as much information about your ideal customer as you can, it's time to summarise the details into one easy-to-understand statement. The more clear and specific you are, the more likely you are to get what you want.

When you can summarise your ideal customer in one clear statement, you and your staff will be perfectly placed to find more of them. Everything you do –

buying products, marketing, selling and even the way you display your products in store or on your website – will be done with your target customer in mind. When that customer is looking for products and services, they will be drawn to you because your business will reflect what is important and relevant to them.

A picture paints a thousand words, so take some time to visualise what your ideal customer looks like, or cut and paste some images of your ideal customer. Consider them as real people. They may be customers you already know, or perhaps they're someone you would like to have as your ideal customer. Either way, do everything you can to personalise them. They are like you and me. They have feelings and problems just like everyone else. The more personal you make them, the more real they will become, and as a result you will create a bond with them even before they become your customer.

When you've completed your customer profile picture and you've answered the questions suggested in the 'Create a customer profile' section of this chapter, your profile statement may be similar to this example:

'My ideal customer is a well-established business owner

or professional. They live in an affluent part of town and have a large discretionary income. They like to furnish their home with quality goods that reflect their status and aspirations. They value expert advice and insights and are willing to pay a reasonable price for what they want.' Now that you have a clear idea of your target customer, you can disregard anyone who is not your target customer. That may sound a bit mean at first, but let's consider what will happen if you don't.

All businesses have limited time and resources. If you continue to spend large portions of your time on the wrong customer, you will continue to get the same results. I am not saying that you ignore customers who are outside of your ideal customer profile, but focus your time, energy and money on your target market.

I recently went through a major overhaul of my business. My team and I redefined our customers into A class (ideal customers) and B class (the rest), and we realised that we were spending a disproportionate amount of time with B class customers. Now our time and energy are focused on A class customers. We still give our B class customers a great service, but we don't waste time looking for more of them.

With a description of your ideal customer, you can now have a look at your current customer base and calculate what percentage represents your ideal customer. If the answer is 10% or lower, then you will need to do some serious prospecting for more target customers.

When you have a clear idea of your ideal customer, everything changes and you will feel energised and inspired to find more of them.

STONE ONE SUMMARY

In Stone One we learned how vital it is to create a customer profile of our ideal customer. We gained an understanding of what is important to them and how to focus our research on their needs and wants, and not our products or services. We learned to take time to define what business we are really in from the perspective of our customers, and we created a profile statement describing our ideal customer.

When you have done this, you will be ready for Stone Two – How To Create A Compelling Message.

1. Maslow, A. H. (n.d.), *Understanding Human Motivation*, 26–47. doi:10.1037/11305–004

2. Theodore Levitt, 'Marketing Myopia', *Harvard Business Review*, 1960

3. Alex Brownsell, *'Furniture retail and DIY Brands switch from price-led to emotive ad strategy'*, 22 March 2012 *www.campaignlive.co.uk* (accessed June 2017)

HOW TO CREATE A COMPELLING MESSAGE

In the 2008 Presidential Election, Barack Obama's research team built a social profile of his 'customer' and identified that most potential voters wanted change. With this in mind, they created a powerful message that could be seen everywhere – on T-shirts, badges, posters, TV and social media.

When Obama spoke, he repeatedly talked about the need for change and captured voters' imagination with his slogan 'Change we can believe in' and the chant 'Yes we can'. The campaign understood that voters were buying into the idea of the need for change, and that Obama was the man to help them achieve it.

With a powerful and compelling message, you can clearly show your customers how your products and services will benefit them personally. It will differentiate you from your competition and answer the question, 'Why should I buy from you?' And it will include a call to action. A well-crafted message will also inspire customers to become advocates for your business, so it needs to be clear and concise so it's easy for them to share with their friends and family.

THE POWER OF WORDS

Since the dawn of time, words have been used to persuade individuals and nations to rally behind great causes, win prestigious tournaments, conquer evil empires and buy iconic products ('Because you're worth it'). In 2005, Steve Jobs inspired students at Stanford University with his 'You've got to find what you love' speech. Sir Winston Churchill rallied an entire nation to carry on against impossible odds with his deeply moving speech 'We shall defend our island, whatever the cost may be... we shall never surrender'.

Jim Telfer electrified the 1997 Lions rugby team with

his 'This is your Everest' speech. At the time, South Africa were world champions, and for good reason. Telfer explained that very few people get the chance in rugby terms to get to the top of their Everest. He reminded the players that being picked for the team was the easy bit, and unless they put their bodies on the line, they wouldn't win, saying, 'If you put in the performance, you'll get what you deserve[1].'

Jim Telfer's inspirational pre-match talk was enough to inspire the Lions to victory.

When David saw how paralysed the men of Israel were in the face of the taunting Goliath, he reminded them of their purpose with five simple words: 'Is there not a cause?' And then he did what all great leaders do: he led by example. Words on their own can be inspiring and uplifting. Words that are supported with action will invariably inspire others to action.

Your words and messages are being communicated every day to your customers. When they enter your store, visit your website or follow you on social media, they are reading or listening to your message. Does your message inspire them to want to know more, or do they become disinterested and switch off? Does your ideal customer clearly understand what you do and what you represent? Does your message move them to action, or do you sound like everyone else?

Having the right message is essential for you to grow your business and increase your turnover. Aim it at your ideal customer and repeat it endlessly on various platforms until it becomes a part of who you are. When you have a clear message about your products and services, you will attract more of the right kind of customers. They will know exactly what you do and what you don't do, and they will have a clear idea of what to expect when they enter your store or buy from you on the internet. Your message will cut through the media noise and resonate with your target customer.

When I was working in Cape Town, I travelled to work by train. I would make my way through the hustle and bustle of commuters, and every morning I would hear the shoe shine boy. Train terminals can be noisy places, but this clever boy would say in an audible whisper, 'Shoe shine! Shoe shine!' Somehow his whisper cut through the loud cries of the other vendors and people would take notice, and he was always busy.

How can you 'whisper' your message (metaphorically) so it is heard by your customer? Getting the right message to your intended audience is a skill that influential men and woman throughout history have spent many hours refining and perfecting.

Your message is not a sales pitch, and it is not intended to coerce your customers into buying something they don't want. The purpose of your message is to help your customers understand in a short space of time what you are good at and what they can expect if they decide to buy from you. Never sell your company and products as something they're not. Customers will appreciate you for your honesty.

In 1960, Volkswagen created a message to change people's perceptions not only about a product, but also about themselves. At that time, Americans were in the habit of buying big American cars and were not interested in small German cars. To counter this thinking, Volkswagen launched its 'Think small' campaign, with adverts for the Beetle emphasising how small it was. The campaign was created by the company Doyle Dane Bernbach and was a runaway success[2]. It didn't try and convince the audience that

Volkswagen was something it wasn't, and customers were able to see the advantages and cost benefits of driving a small and trendy car.

Dove beauty products created a message based around the 'Real Beauty' campaign – 'Imagine a world where beauty is a source of confidence, not anxiety'. The message was sensitive but meaningful to its customers.

For example, Dove's Real Beauty Sketches campaign created messages around a social experiment in which an FBI-trained sketch artist was asked to draw female volunteers twice – first as each woman described herself, and the second time as a random stranger described her. The second image was always more beautiful and positive than the image described by the women themselves. Dove supported this finding with a compelling statistic that only 4% of woman around the world consider themselves beautiful[3].

I love this example from Dove because it shows that the company cares. When you genuinely care about your customers, it will show. And it will show in your message.

I worked with a retailer a few years ago who had a stunning showroom with a large display window on a busy high street. They had everything going for them. But whenever I visited them, I saw the way they treated their customers. They didn't care about their customers, and in fact were sometimes quite rude. Needless to say, they are no longer in business.

At the other end of the spectrum, I was speaking to Sunny from LED Wholesale recently. He had won a big order to supply in-store lighting for a large department store. The first phase of the order was meant to be delivered to a new store in Glasgow, but due to circumstances out of his control, it arrived too late for the courier to meet the deadline. Without hesitation, he and his wife jumped in their car and travelled five hours to deliver the lights themselves. When the store manager heard what they had done, he insisted on paying for a hotel for them to stay in overnight. Sunny and his wife literally went the extra mile.

What can you do to go the extra mile for your customers? How is your business different and unique? What weaknesses do you have that could be turned to your customers' advantage? How can you show that you care?

MESSAGES THAT TURN CUSTOMERS OFF

When you craft your message, be careful not to repeat tired and worn phrases that are used by the masses. For example, most companies claim to have the 'highest quality' and the 'best service', but this is the minimum that customers expect and doesn't differentiate you from your competitors.

Avoid clichés and hackneyed phrases such as 'We are leaders in our field', 'We are customer-focused', 'We sell state-of-the-art products with leading edge technology', 'We're your experienced team of professionals', and my personal favourite 'We pride ourselves on our...'

Be original.
Be thoughtful.
Be engaging and memorable.

THREE STEPS TO CREATING THE RIGHT MESSAGE

A powerful message will have purpose and clarity and will convince others that you and your products are what they will need to solve their problems. Having the right message will also provide you and your staff with a clear vision and inspire you to excellence. Your message will define who you are, what your business is about and why you are in business.

We learned how to create a customer profile in Stone One. Now we will learn how to create a compelling message that will appeal to your ideal customer.

What do you stand for? What cause are you prepared to dedicate your time and effort to? Before you can create the right message, you will need to dig deep down to the roots of who you are and why you are doing what you do. Your message should be alive and vibrant, making you and your staff proud to tell others about it. Ideally, you will be able to recite it not just from memory, but from your heart. When your message comes from your heart, it will have a lasting impact on your customers.

Your message needs to be sincere. If you attempt to say anything that just sounds nice, or you create a message that you don't really believe in, your customers will sense your insincerity. Ralph Waldo Emerson summed it up like this: 'What you do speaks so loud that I cannot hear what you say'. In other words, what you say and what you do need to be the same.

I am sure there have been times when someone has made you a promise, and even while they were speaking, you had the uneasy feeling that they were unlikely to follow it through. You couldn't quite put your finger on it, but you knew they were being insincere. If you are saying something that is not entirely honest, people will know. Be genuine.

Let's have a look at the three steps to help you build your powerful message.

Step 1 – What is the benefit to your customer?
No-one is going to change their buying behaviours until they believe that there is a big enough reason to do so.

The status quo is your enemy. I used the same stationer on the High Street for eighteen years and only stopped because it closed down – it's a pity the owners didn't get a chance to read my book! I've had the same hairdresser for the past four years and the same accountant for seven years. They are doing a great job and they charge a reasonable price. I'm sure I could get the same services at a lower price if I shopped around, but it's just too much hassle.

When we are comfortable, familiar and happy with the status quo, we don't change. People are more likely to change their behaviour when there is an external reason to do so. Most people get defensive when they are told that they are the problem, but they become engaged when they are told that something or someone else has created a problem or opportunity for them to tackle. That's why it's usually easier for the political party out of power to establish a platform for change. It can always blame the party in power when things are not going well.

In retail, manufacturers can target the current status quo by pointing out its weaknesses. James Dyson invented a revolutionary new vacuum cleaner in 1983 that eventually sold millions. He was able to persuade customers to upgrade to a Dyson because they didn't need to continually purchase replacement bags. At the time, the UK Market for disposable bags was £100 million. The slogan 'Say goodbye to the bag' proved a hit with the buying public[4] because customers were prepared to pay extra for a vacuum cleaner for the convenience of not having to change the dust bag.

Independent retailers are in a strong position to compete with giant online retailers and the national chains when it comes to creating their messages. You know your local market and so your message can be more personal to your customers' needs. Your message should highlight the advantages of your expert personal advice, products and services that are tailored to customers' specific needs. You are not a 'one size fits all' retailer, unlike the giants. Make sure that your message includes these differences.

Step 2 – Why should they buy from you?

Imagine a real customer is in your store or visiting your website, about to make a decision whether to buy what you sell. What would motivate them to buy your product? What will it do for them? How will it improve their lives? How is your business different from your competitors'? How will your customer be better off buying from you rather than buying from others? What does your business do better and what doesn't it do?

Make an inventory of your products and services and consider how they are of benefit to your customers. Don't make assumptions here. It's worth taking the time to interview your customers either one-to-one or via a short survey. Review what they are saying on social media and make notes of any key words. Write down all the good that your company does – not just the great products you sell, but how you treat your customers, whether they buy or not. How do you look after your staff and what contributions do you make to your community? Are you known for giving great service and for going the extra mile? Do you give excellent after-sales service or offer special guarantees?

How are you different from your competitors? What makes you unique? At first glance it may appear to your customers that you're just the same as everyone else. I remember how deflated I felt when customers would tell me that the lights in my catalogue were the same as my competitors'. It was difficult to disagree because they did look similar. It was only after I did a careful analysis of my products that I was able to point out the differences and advantages of my products compared to the competition.

When you know what makes you unique and how your products and services can benefit your customers, your confidence increases. You are no longer on the back foot, defending your existence. Instead you are gently leaning in. Your advice makes sense and your customer can clearly see the benefits of buying from you rather than your competition.

Professional tennis players regularly consult with their coaches to discuss their strengths and weaknesses. They may have a strong serve, an excellent forehand and a great drop shot, but if they ignore the fact that their backhand is weak, they will never reach their full potential. You have to know what your strengths and weaknesses are so that you can emphasise your strengths and work on your weaknesses. You also need to know what your strengths and weaknesses are relative to your competition. Only then can you differentiate your business and provide concrete reasons for customers to flock to your store.

Step 3 – What actions do you want customers to take?
The obvious answer would be for them to buy your products. That's probably true in most cases, but depending on your industry, they may need to take a few smaller steps before they buy your core products or services. For example, an interior designer may want clients to agree to a free consultation in their home in order to make recommendations. If you don't tell your target audience what action you want them to take through social media, on your website or in store, don't be surprised if they don't take any action at all.

In the marketing world, asking your customer or prospect to do something is known as a 'call to action' (CTA). That something may be signing up for your newsletter or subscribing to your Facebook page. It may be buying a product while it's on special offer, or it may mean completing a short survey so you can help customers find the products that are important to them.

Whether it's 'Buy now because there is a limited offer' or 'Sign up now to receive my 10 tips on how to dress like a celebrity', your call to action needs to be loud and clear. Your end goal is for your customer to buy your products and be happy with their purchase. These smaller action steps are designed to be helpful and informative, but should lead to your ideal customer buying their ideal products from you.

There are three criteria for effective CTAs whether online, in store or in a mail-shot:

1. A no-obligation statement that removes or at least reduces any risk.
This is particularly effective if you are offering a free trial rather than a purchase, i.e. 'Try us and we're sure you'll like what we have to offer'. This gives customers the confidence to buy after the trial.

I recently signed up for a free three-month trial with iTunes that allows me to download a massive amount of music for free. After the trial, I agree to pay a monthly fee or cancel the subscription. I was hesitant to sign up initially as I spend more time listening to audiobooks than music, but as it was a free trial I decided to take the plunge. I am now loving listening to great music past and present and will struggle to cancel this subscription when the free trial has ended. This CTA certainly hooked me, and it looks like iTunes has another customer.

2. Click the button.

Tell people what to do next. In most cases, you are asking them to click the button on your website so they can accept your offer, but this principle also applies to a reply card that they can either post or complete in store. Either way, the instruction needs to be clear and easy to process.

As I am writing this paragraph, I have just received an email from the *Retail Gazette* which is an industry magazine I subscribe to. The email is promoting a conference in Copenhagen for retailers to attend or exhibit at. At the bottom of the email is a series of CTA buttons for me to click, depending on my interest. This is a perfect example of making it easy for customers to take action.

3. Encourage customers to respond immediately.

Since the launch of the first mail order company in 1845, marketers have learned the importance of getting people to take action straight away. Don't give your customers the option to wait and think about it. We live in a world of distractions and it's far too easy to lose concentration. Make it as easy as possible for them to take action, and encourage them to act now.

I recently received an email about a new business book that I have been looking forward to reading. The email invited me to take advantage of a special price by downloading the book now, or pay a higher price if I waited. It also offered me a free paperback version if I wrote a review on Amazon within seven days. Of course, I downloaded the book there and then and will post a review shortly.

SHARE, REVIEW, REVISE AND POLISH

A good message should be punchy, have defined objectives, serve multiple functions and be long lasting. This editing part of the process is worth every effort to get it right. Share it with others whose opinion you value. Ask them if it makes sense and inspires them. Make any further adjustments until you and your staff are happy with the result. Don't worry if it's not perfect, as your message will evolve over time. When you are convinced that your message represents who you are and what your business is, create a shorter, punchier version.

When Martin Luther King delivered his speech on ending racism and called for equal civil and economic rights, he spoke with passion and the belief that his cause was just and vital for the minority groups who were disadvantaged and downtrodden. However, the reason that his speech is so memorable is because he refined it with three simple words, 'I have a dream', which he repeated over and over. It resonated with everyone listening at the time, and still stirs emotions when people hear it more than fifty years later.

For maximum impact, you will need two versions of your message. The first message will have enough detail for your customers to gain sufficient insight to make an informed decision about you. It will also include a call to action.

The second version will be shorter and punchier and must be delivered in one or two sentences, maximum. This second version could become your company slogan for use on your website, social media, signage and stationary. The main advantage of a slogan is that it helps your customers identify with you and clearly describes what your business is about. A good slogan will also be memorable.

When you have a clear and compelling message that you believe in, watch how it makes a difference in your business. It's like turning on a light switch. Your customers are no longer seen as people to sell to in order to reach your daily sales targets. You will see them as people you care about – genuinely, not superficially. You will be able to see them as having real problems that you can help them with, and you will see the problems from their point of view.

Let's have a look at how the right message has made a difference to some well known companies. Ikea is known for producing trendy and affordable furniture focused on making everyday life better for its customers rather than trying to convince customers how great its products are.

eBay's mission is to 'provide a global trading platform where practically anyone can trade practically anything'. I love this catchy slogan, but I also love the fact that eBay gives sellers 'the platform, solutions and support they need to grow their businesses and thrive'[5]. Of course, eBay is a business and its aim is to make money and be profitable, but there is more to business than just making money. eBay's message goes on to say,

'We measure our success by our customers' success.' The focus is clearly on its customers.

If your focus is primarily on making money, your customers will sense it and will be wary of your advice. When you genuinely care about your customers' buying experience, they are more likely to listen to you and act on your recommendations.

Your message and slogan should inspire you to act beyond your normal abilities and leap beyond your potential. The dictionary defines inspiration as 'breathing in; an inspiring or animating action or influence; a divine influence directly and immediately exerted upon the mind or soul'[6]. If your message includes some or all of these qualities then you are ready to leapfrog your business into a new and exciting era. You will have a reason for opening your doors to your customers each day and will be positive and enthusiastic. The right message helps you to find meaning in your work. William Pollard, who grew ServiceMaster into a worldwide company, sums this up in his book *The Soul of the Firm* by saying, 'People want to work for a cause, not just a living[7].'

STONE TWO SUMMARY

In Stone Two we learned how to create a compelling message by using the power of words.

With the right message, you will attract more of the right kind of customers to your business. When your message is clear, it will cut through the media noise and resonate with your customers.

There are three steps to creating a powerful message. Firstly, what is the benefit to your customer? Secondly, why should they buy from you? And thirdly, what actions do you want them to take?

Once you have your perfect message, you need to share, review, revise and polish it and then launch it into the world.

1. Jim Telfer, Everest speech. https://youtu.be/kM0dx0h2xsw

2. 'Ad Age Advertising Century: Top 100 Campaigns', Crain Communications Inc. March 29, 1999. adage.com.

3. www.dove.com/Real-Beauty

4. James Dyson – Wikipedia

5. www.ebayinc.com/Company Information

6. www.dictionary.com

7. Pollard, C. W, *The Soul Of The Firm*. New York: C Grant and Company, 2010, page 45

THE PRODUCT ECOSYSTEM

Once you know who your ideal customer is and you have a well-crafted message, you need to ensure you are able to provide great products and services that match their expectations. This is known as the product ecosystem, which is more than just selling products.

There are three elements to the product ecosystem that will help your customers make a real connection with you and your business. The first element is your product's ability to appeal to your customers' emotional needs. The second is the physical aspect of the actual product, and the third element is the digital impact of your products or services.

With the rise of the internet, customers have a myriad of choices. They are also well informed and can price check at the touch of a button. This makes your life even more challenging than ever and there are times when you may lose the will to live! That's understandable – I know how frustrating it can be as I speak with retailers who have this same problem every day.

And yet there is a solution. It will require a different mindset, and you will need to develop a product ecosystem that will be attractive and desirable to your target customer. When you place your customers' needs at the heart of the sale, they are more likely to see how your products can solve their problem or satisfy a need.

WHAT IS THE PRODUCT ECOSYSTEM?

I couldn't find a suitable definition of a product ecosystem and so I have created my own. When the three elements of emotion, physical products and digital media support and lead your customers to purchase your core products or services, you have a product ecosystem.

In nature, we think of an ecosystem as a community of living organisms that live in conjunction and harmony with each other. A plant cannot survive on its own and is reliant on the air, water, nutrients in the soil and other living organisms to flourish and grow. Similarly, your core products cannot survive in isolation and require a product ecosystem to thrive.

Core products are the higher priced products that you want to be known for and sell on a regular basis. The value of your core product will vary depending on your industry, but the key is to have a range of core products that will provide significant margins and can be sold frequently.

The definition of 'frequently' will vary from retailer to retailer. If one of your core products is a Ferrari, then you may be happy to make a sale once a month. For lower priced core products, you may need to sell two or three a week. If you sell low priced products, you may need to sell a special package of smaller items that make up a core offer. However you define your core products, it is important to identify what they are so that you can create a product ecosystem to help support them.

Let's discus the three elements that support your core products – emotional, physical and digital – in more detail.

EMOTIONAL

The emotional part of the ecosystem refers to your products' ability to appeal to your customers' emotional needs. Different products will have different appeals, but there is always an emotional reason why customers buy them, even if they are not aware of it.

Luxury items will appeal to their need for status or to be recognised. People don't buy a Ferrari just because it's fast. When someone is considering a new kitchen, they don't just want a room with drawers and cupboards to keep things in, nor do they just want an oven that cooks. They want something that will look great, make them feel inspired and be inviting and welcoming to their family and friends.

People buy products to reflect their personality and satisfy their creative needs. At heart, we are all creators, and we cherish the opportunity to create new environments that will uplift and edify.

Do you remember how much fun you had when you first learned to splash paint on a sketch pad or created your first piece of pottery at school? I remember making a very distorted ashtray out of clay for my dad in primary school. I loved getting my hands messy, but my favourite part was painting and varnishing it when it had hardened. I didn't care that my dad didn't even smoke because I was having so much fun.

Whether you are selling clothes, furniture, jewellery, toys or beds, you are a co-creator with your customer. Don't hinder their creativity by selling them a product or a thing. Help them to tap into their creative juices by facilitating the process. Ask them about their home or garden and what they hope will happen when they buy your product. Be an artist and paint a picture for them of how the item they select will look and make them feel, as if it was already in their lives. Have fun. The more fun you have and the more creative you can be with your customer, the more you will appeal to their positive emotions.

Other products may appeal to your customers' desire to belong, such as fashionable clothing or accessories. People used to buy Volvos because of their emotional need to feel safe when driving, and most people buy insurance for peace of mind.

We also buy products based on our emotional need for familiarity. I remember going to a pharmacy recently to buy a box of headache tablets. I asked for a well-known brand because I was familiar with it and I trusted the company which produced the tablets. However, the pharmacist suggested that I buy the cheaper non-branded product because it had exactly the same ingredients. Even though she was a trained pharmacist and knew what she was talking about, I hesitated. Reluctantly I bought the cheaper non-branded tablets and they worked well. However, a few months later, I went back to buying the well-known brand which I had built a connection with over many years.

When you uncover the emotional connection that your customer has with your core products, you will do less selling and more facilitating. In other words, you will help them to make the decision that is right for them.

I have learned from forty years of selling that our job is not to manipulate or trick people into buying our core products. Instead, we are there to listen, advise, create and provide the best possible solution or product to satisfy their emotional desires. Each customer will have different needs, so focus on what is important to them. There is no point in trying to sell someone a sofa based on how great it looks if all they are interested in is how comfortable it is. Ask questions and listen.

A few years ago, my wife and I were house hunting and we looked at some wonderful homes. We gave the estate agent a list of our criteria and requested that our new home be in a quiet location. I remember being shown a beautiful home with a big garden that ticked all the boxes, except that it was on a busy road. No matter how fantastic the house was, the quiet area was crucial to us since I'm a light sleeper.

PHYSICAL

The physical element refers to the actual products or services that support or lead customers to your core products. It is tangible in the sense that you can clearly see the product or explain its service features.

The core product for a financial advisor could be life insurance. We can't actually see it or touch it, but we all know what it means. The physical products that support the life insurer's core product could be brochures, marketing campaigns, a life insurance monthly premium calculator or a free gift for prompt action.

Consumers are becoming more and more demanding when it comes to quality and presentation. They expect perfection, from the box the item is kept in to the product itself. Presentation is vital and your showroom should display your products in the best way possible.

I have a customer who provides incentive's to her staff to replace blown lamps so their lighting displays always look great. Another customer told me that he was unable to sell a table lamp to a customer because he had opened the box to show the previous customer the colour.

What are your core products, and what lower priced products could support or lead your customers to them? How can you present your products in a way that will be appealing and attractive to your customers?

DIGITAL

Digital media has become a part of our everyday life. As an independent retailer, you likely already know the value of having a good website. While results may vary, a basic website that showcases your store is essential for any good business.

Digital media is a platform on which you can market and sell your products and promote your services via your website, podcasts, YouTube, Facebook, LinkedIn and so on. We will go into more detail about the various digital media platforms in Stone Five – You Are The Brand.

I strongly recommend that your digital media campaign is supported with printed material, such as brochures and catalogues. When digital media was first introduced, many suppliers decided to replace their catalogues with digital images. While this worked for customers who were dedicated online shoppers, it failed to make sales for in-store buyers. They loved to see the products on show, but they also liked the option of flipping through full colour catalogues. Suppliers quickly learned the importance of having up to date printed brochures as well as digital images.

If you are reliant on customers buying your products only when they are in your showroom, then you will not be around very long. Most retailers will have a website showcasing their products, their location and what their business is about. Some will have an e-commerce website so that their customers can buy online.

All this is the minimum requirement for you to succeed and sell products, but it is not enough. You need to develop a connection and a relationship with your customers, even when they are not in your showroom.

Social media began as a place to share photos and experiences with friends and family. Since then it has grown into a worldwide phenomenon with millions of users, and it's now used to share ideas, showcase products and services, and to launch worthwhile campaigns. If you want to sell more products and services, this is where you need to be. Ironically, though, your primary goal will not be to try and sell your products through social media. People go on to social media to socialise, so if your primary focus is to sell them something, they will shut you down.

Content is key, and we will discuss this in more detail in Stone 5. Your primary goal on social media is to create an ongoing connection with your customers or prospects. Your content should be informative and instructive and designed to help improve their lives. Over time, your customers will develop a positive relationship with you when they see you as the expert in your field. As a guide, share 85% free content and 15% incentives to buy via your website. Remember to make it easy for customers to find your website when you share useful content on social media.

When you provide your customers with free advice or insights to help them solve a problem, they are more likely to read, view or listen to what you have to say. There are some incredible free YouTube training courses to help you buy the right house, purchase a new car, create the right lighting, and even learn how to play the piano.

How would you feel if you got some free advice from an estate agent about where to find your ideal home? If you had a great experience watching or listening to their top tips and you felt you could trust them, you have created a unique relationship with that person. When you are ready to buy your next house, who are you most likely to buy from? There is a good chance that you will buy from the person you have been seeking advice and insights from.

When I was searching for ways to increase my turnover, I read many good business books on the subject. However, when I read Daniel Priestley's books *Oversubscribed*[1] and *Key Person of Influence*[2], I felt a connection. I then watched his website's tips and lessons on YouTube about how to become a key player in my industry, and I don't mind admitting that I became a little obsessed. I would watch every interview, blog or training video that he posted many times. By the time I finally got to shake his hand at his training workshop – along with the fifty other delegates – I felt like we were best buddies. I am grateful for the lessons I learned from him, and I look forward to learning from other inspiring business leaders in the future.

What lessons or tips can you freely share with your customers without making your products the centre of your digital campaign? A garden centre could go to town providing tips on gardening. A bakery could supply endless advice on how to bake great cakes. If you own a clothing store, how about giving free fashion advice and providing insights into upcoming trends?

As I look out my window from my office, I am reminded that I need to paint our fence. Do I spray or paint?

I've just gone on Google and there is some great advice on how to paint a fence and the advantages and disadvantages of spraying or painting. There are even videos I can watch. Now I'm not saying I will definitely buy the paint from the store which gave the best tips, but there is a high probability that I will.

Now would be a great time to review your product ecosystem. Are there any gaps that need filling or improving? Remember to consider each element of your products – emotional, physical and digital – so that they work together in harmony.

STEPPING STONES TO YOUR CORE PRODUCTS

What are you known for? What would you like to be known for? If you had a choice, which products or services would you prefer to sell? How can your other products support increased sales of your core product?

When you know what your core offering is, everything else is ancillary, designed to support or provide stepping stones to that product. When I go to a furniture store, it is obvious that its core products are sofas and tables. The side tables, lamps and other accessories on display are mainly there to support and complement the core products, creating a visual effect that helps the customer to picture the core products in their home.

Free or lower priced products can be used to lead customers to your core range of products. Imagine a rushing river with your core product on one side and your customer on the other. The customer can vaguely make out your product in the distance, and although it looks great, they are still not sure. They could try to wade through the river, but it looks dangerous and they don't want to make a big mistake. If you genuinely want to help, you get your expert staff to place a series of stepping stones across the river so that your customer can get a good look at your core product and make an informed choice.

The river represents the customer's doubts and fears about which products to buy or whom to buy them from. The stepping stones represent your free or low value products, such as a blog, YouTube video or Facebook article, that help your customer to develop trust in you. When I say low value, I mean in price. If you get this right, they should be of high worth to the customer, even if they are free.

When my wife and I decided to buy a bigger home, we needed more space for my office, family and friends and future grandchildren. Our daughter was getting married that year and I knew that we would need to be super-organised if we were going to enjoy a smooth transition.

We looked at a few wonderful houses in the area, but when we made an offer, we found that the process of selling our house and buying the new home was lengthy and complicated. Fortunately for us, there was a range of luxury houses being built only two miles from where we had lived for many years. We viewed the excellent photos and videos on the website and researched details of the building company and its products. The website gave good advice about what to look for in a property and how easy it would be to part-exchange our home. With the time pressure we were under, we decided it was worth checking out the properties.

The sales representative guided us around a well-designed showroom, and then on to our future home that was just a shell at that point. She then illustrated what our house could look like using a series of wonderful brochures and explained the process to buying our ideal home. Given our time restraints, we jumped at this opportunity. I am pleased to say that it only took two months from our first viewing to moving in, and we have beautiful photos from the morning of our daughter's wedding as she left from our new home.

What principles can you learn from this story that could be applied to your products and services? In our case, the raging river we faced was the time restraint. We also had genuine fears about the process of buying a new house.

The low value products – the stepping stones – that helped us purchase our new home were the free online advice, photos and videos. We were also given additional stepping stones by the representative with the brochure and advice. All of these helped us to walk across the raging river one step at a time until we joyfully received the keys to our brand new home.

Are you getting some ideas of what stepping stones you will need to help your customers walk across the river to your core product or service? You may want to take a moment to write these ideas down while they are fresh in your mind. I would encourage you to produce brochures with not only pictures of your products, but also how you will guide your customer across the river step by step with advice and services so that they will make the right buying decision for them.

WHAT CUSTOMERS WILL PAY

Customers will pay you what they think your products are worth, not what they are actually worth. With the right product ecosystem, you can influence their thinking by demonstrating your value and expertise.

The reason retailers sell products at big discounts has less to do with price matching and more to do with the value that they place on themselves. If your starting point is to match or beat any price, then that's exactly what your customers will expect. However, if your purpose is to provide added value and expertise, then it's vital that you tell your customers before they begin the buying process.

You have a wealth of experience that can help guide your customers to make a buying decision that will be of great worth to them. The problem is that customers won't always appreciate your value if you don't tell them. With your guidance, they can avoid making mistakes that they will regret and that other customers have made.

We live in a fast-moving consumer world, and surfing the net and clicking on a few buttons may not always be the customer's best solution. The reason customers enter your store is because they want to see and feel the products before they make a purchase. Depending on what you sell, many of them will want advice before they buy. But what value do you put on your expertise?

Before the internet, your customers valued your time and expertise, and demonstrated this by purchasing the products from you because you helped them make the right decision. Today, customers under-value your time and expertise. They are happy to receive your guidance, but are not prepared to pay for it. In other words, once you have helped them find what they are looking for, they blatantly buy the same item online at a lower price.

The only reason they will do this is if you allow them to do it. Now is the time to stop devaluing your expertise and help your customers appreciate it.

How do you demonstrate your value to your customers to the point that they will pay you what you are worth? This can be done in a few minutes, but it needs to be done at the beginning of the sale, before you begin a discussion about their purchase. Before you can demonstrate your value, though, you need to do some homework. You need to understand and identify your target customer's dominant problems. If they only have a slight problem, then they are unlikely to need your advice.

For example, if you wanted to buy a pair of shoes and you knew what colour, size and make you needed, you probably wouldn't need a sales assistant to help you pick out the right ones. You would simply tell them what you wanted and they would check the stock and bring you the shoes. However, if you didn't know which shoes you needed or what size or make, you may need a little more help. If you also needed a new dress and a matching handbag or a new suit, shirt and tie, you would probably appreciate some expert advice.

What are the problems associated with making a purchase from your store? What are some of the frustrations that cause customers a headache? What are common mistakes that customers make in your industry? What negative buying experiences have they had in the past?

Here are some of the silly mistakes that customers make in the lighting industry, and they are so common, it's laughable. They forget to measure the height of their ceiling and then purchase a chandelier that's too big for their room. With so many variations in light output in LED lighting these days, customers will often install a fitting that doesn't give sufficient light. Most customers want to dim their lights, but some LED fittings are not dimmable and others need a specific dimmer, depending on the light. If customers get this wrong, they can blow the fitting, which can be an expensive mistake for them. Lighting retailers who help customers avoid these mistakes are more likely to win the sale. Provided they have the right discussion before the sale begins. Make a list of all the problems and pitfalls that customers face when making a purchase. Now, prioritise the list to target three common problems that your products and services can solve. You may want to refer back to your list from 'Why should they buy from you?' in Stone Two. In the lighting example, the customer wants a light that is the right size, gives sufficient light output and can be dimmed without blowing the lights. The clearer you are about your target market's dominant problems, the easier it is for you to solve them.

When you have identified the dominant problems in your industry, the common mistakes customers make and you know what results they want your products to deliver, you need to make a brochure which includes all of these. The more creative and colourful your brochure, the greater the impact.

The purpose of the brochure is to help your customers make the right buying decision and pay you what you are worth. Whenever you have a customer who needs your time and expertise, show them your brochure and talk them through the three steps. Explain to them the common problems and mistakes that other people have made and how you can help them avoid these pitfalls. And then show them examples of happy customers who took your advice and were pleased with the results. Help them to value your expertise by telling them about your experience and any awards you have won relevant to your industry. Give them an overview of your core products and how you will help them to find the ones that will suit their specific needs. The more you can demonstrate your expertise and credibility, the more they will trust you.

Now comes the difficult part, but it's vital that you do this at the beginning of the sale to avoid any misunderstanding. Explain that you will do everything within your power to help them avoid these mistakes and buy the right products for their needs. Then explain that your time is valuable and you will need to be paid for it. However, you will not be charging them a fee for your advice. Instead, all you ask is for them to pay a reasonable price for the products or services they buy. In other words, you won't be matching any internet prices. Then ask them if they are happy to go ahead on this basis.

If they agree to go ahead then you can proceed, confident that you will make a sale with reasonable margins. Of course, there will be some customers who will renege on your agreement, but most of them will be happy to pay the price.

Now I realise how confrontational this may sound, and it can be difficult to do in the beginning. But it is worth persisting as it will get easier the more you practise. It may seem like explaining this process will take a long time, but we are only talking about a few minutes. And these are the most valuable few minutes of the entire sale. When your customer understands how they will benefit from your expertise, they are more likely to support you and buy from you at a sensible price.

The examples that I have discussed have been for bricks and mortar stores, but the principles can also apply to internet retailers. This is especially effective when there is a dialogue between you and your customer. The process is the same, but it may take place over the phone or via email.

FINDING THE RIGHT SUPPLIERS

Of course, it is not possible to have a product ecosystem with core products if you don't have great suppliers. Selecting the right suppliers is essential to ensure that you are able to deliver your products and services on time, at the right price and quality. As an independent striving to become a specialist retailer, you also need a level of exclusivity, and if possible a selective distribution channel. A selective distribution is where a supplier agrees to supply retailers who meet certain criteria.

For example, a selective distribution supplier may agree to only supply bricks and mortar retailers, as long as the retailer agrees to display a certain quantity of their products. This is legal, and is a great way to fight off the giant online retailers as they will be unable to sell products from this supplier.

There are four key points that you will need to consider when selecting your suppliers:

1. Selection criteria.
Create a list of criteria that suppliers need to meet or fulfil. This could include the following:

- Lead times from receipt of your order to delivery
- Minimum and maximum order quantities
- Cost of carriage
- Quality control processes

- Payment terms and conditions
- Discount policies
- Returns procedure
- Contactable references

When you set the criteria in advance, you are in a stronger position to evaluate potential suppliers on each of them and you can avoid any costly mistakes in the future. This may seem a bit strange at first as usually suppliers run checks on their potential customers, not the other way around. You need to see how good their quality control is, what stock levels they maintain, what their after sales service is like. It's too late when you are stuck with a faulty product and an angry customer and your supplier is not playing ball. It's your reputation that will be tarnished if there's a problem, not theirs.

2. Define your process.

Identify the process that you will use to find suitable suppliers. There are some great trade shows where you can find a wide range of suppliers.

In my industry, we have exhibitions in Birmingham, Frankfurt and Milan, and I am always amazed at the vast range of products and suppliers available.

However, trade shows can be overwhelming, especially when there are so many suppliers and endless halls to visit. It's worth doing your homework before you go so you can spend most of your time with suppliers who match your criteria.

You may also want to allocate a time frame to spend with each supplier and make appointments where you can. If someone else in your business also attends, you could separate for a time and then compare notes over lunch. As a specialist retailer, you want to find niche products and that will take time, so the more prepared you are, the better your chances of finding that special supplier.

3. Selective distribution.

It's crucial to get as many selective distribution suppliers as you can. If possible, link up with other retailers in your industry to help negotiate with suppliers who are prepared to give you selective distribution. Remind them you will be making a significant investment and that it is in everyone's interest to supply goods in this way. Working with other retailers is particularly helpful when you are looking for new suppliers who are trying to enter your market from overseas. They will be more amenable to this kind of agreement.

I know of a supplier to the bathroom trade who has different discount structures for their bricks-and-mortar retailers and their wholesalers. Because the high street retailers invest big money in displays for their showrooms, they attract a better discount than the wholesaler. This encourages retailers to buy more bathroom supplies from this supplier and discourages wholesalers from undercutting the high street retailer online simply because the latter doesn't have the margins.

4. Monitor supplier performance.
Even the most reliable supplier can occasionally slip up. Make sure you have regular reviews with your supplier and ask them for stockholding and quality control (QC) reports so you can see the percentage of damaged and faulty goods relative to their overall sales. Some suppliers will keep QC problems as a closely guarded secret and you only find out about them when it's too late. If a supplier's quality is slipping, you need to know so you can make any adjustments, perhaps by discontinuing certain problem lines.

There are significant advantages in having a good relationship with your suppliers. I have seen suppliers bend over backwards for customers who have built good relationships with them. By contrast, I have also seen suppliers give poor service to customers they don't like. We really are in the people-to-people business.

STONE THREE SUMMARY

Just as plants can't survive without water, nutrients and sunlight, your products need a healthy ecosystem to thrive. Your product ecosystem should include the three elements of emotion, physical products and digital media to support and lead your customers to purchase your core products or services.

Customers will pay you what they think your products are worth, and if they can get them cheaper on the internet, they will. With a strong range of core products backed up with exceptional service, price matching becomes less of an issue. I have seen too many retailers offering unnecessary discounts even before the customer has asked for them. If you can show your customer the added value you can provide before the sale begins, they will be more willing to pay a reasonable price. However, it is vital that you have this conversation *before* the sales process begins.

I appreciate that some sales are quick and there is no time to explain the benefits of buying from your store. This is usually when the customer knows exactly what they want and how much they are willing to pay. Having a conversation about your added service is only effective when it is clear that your customer needs help and guidance and the sale's process may take hours or even days.

Having great products is important, but having great suppliers is also vital for a healthy product ecosystem. As an independent striving to become a specialist retailer, you need a level of exclusivity and if possible a selective distribution channel. Search for suppliers who will meet your criteria for ongoing good quality and timely deliveries.

When you know what you want in a supplier, you are in a strong position to weed out the chaff and secure those who will provide you with exclusive products and excellent service. Your business will thrive when you have good suppliers.

In most cases, less is better than more. Remember you don't need to be all things to all people. Provide a few products and services in a remarkable way. Customers will always remember great service.

1. Priestley, D. , *Oversubscribed: How to get people lining up to do business with you*. West Sussex, United Kingdom: Capstone, a Wiley brand, 2015.
2. Priestley, D., *Key Person of Influence: The five-step method to become one of the most highly valued and highly paid people in your industry*. Great Britain: Rethink Press, 2014.

The Power
Of Prospecting

Getting the right sale is about selling more of your core products or services on a regular basis to your ideal customer. When you know who your ideal customer is, and you have a compelling message along with great products, you are in an ideal position to target more of them.

A prospect is a person who is not yet a customer but who fits the description of your ideal customer described in Stone One – Who Is Your Ideal Customer? In this chapter we will discuss how to prospect for your ideal customers by applying the principle of digging the well before you thirst. We will review the importance of having a strong database and discuss how to overcome the Goliaths – the fears that may be preventing you from actively prospecting for new business.

Prospecting for new business is the number one fear for most salespeople. And yet it's the most financially rewarding. In this context, prospecting means one-to-one phone calls or face-to-face canvassing for new business, ideally from a well sourced referral. Advertising in local magazines and on other media platforms has its advantages, but person-to-person prospecting is a powerful low-cost method of attracting great customers. The big advantage is that most independent retailers don't use this method and are happy to sit and wait for customers to come to them. When you choose this method of prospecting, you immediately rise above your competitors.

FLECKS OF GOLD

There was a young merchant from Boston who was caught up in the Californian gold rush of 1848. He sold all of his possessions to seek his fortune in the California rivers, which according to the news were filled with gold nuggets that would make him rich beyond his wildest dreams.

He spent weeks dipping his pan into the river, searching for gold nuggets, but every day he came up empty. His only reward for this exhausting work was a growing pile of rocks. He became discouraged and he was broke.

He was ready to quit when an old, experienced prospector said to him, 'That's quite a pile of rocks you are getting there, young man.'

The merchant replied, 'There is no gold here. I'm going home.'

Walking over to the pile of rocks, the old prospector said, 'Oh, there is gold all right. You just have to know where to find it.' He picked two rocks up and crashed them together. One of the rocks split open, revealing several flecks of gold sparkling in the sunlight.

Noticing a bulging leather pouch fastened to the prospector's waist, the young man said, 'I'm looking for nuggets like the ones in your pouch, not just tiny flecks.'

The old prospector extended his pouch towards the young man, who looked inside, expecting to see several large nuggets. He was stunned to see that the pouch was filled with thousands of flecks of gold.

The old prospector said, 'Son, it seems to me you are so busy looking for large nuggets that you're missing the opportunity to fill your pouch with these precious flecks of gold. The patient accumulation of these little flecks has brought me great wealth[1].'

Effective prospecting requires regular and consistent efforts of gentle probing, inviting and asking. We live in an age with multiple prospecting opportunities such as digital marketing, social media, word of mouth and cold calling. A balanced approach to prospecting will bring you 'flecks of gold' that will over time fill your pouch with customers.

The starting point in prospecting for new business is with your existing customers. If they are happy with your products and services, they are more likely to refer you to their friends. They are also more likely to return to you because of your great service, but you must not be complacent about that. Keep them on your database and invite them back regularly. If you want them to tell their friends about you, give them incentives to do just that.

The best way to incentivise your customers is to give them remarkable service. What does it mean to be remarkable? In his book *Oversubscribed*, Daniel Priestley explains that being remarkable isn't about 'offering stupid gimmicks or pointless stunts' but 'being the best in your niche or micro-niche, offering genuine advantages, real benefits and a superior experience'[2]. It is far better to invest money in making your existing customers' experience remarkable than on traditional forms of advertising.

This may sound counterintuitive, but word of mouth is the most powerful form of advertising, and with social media being prevalent in all of our lives, word of mouth is even more powerful than before. Your customers will say great things about you if you give them an ongoing remarkable experience.

The reality is that you can't give remarkable service to everyone, even if you want to. If you try, you will dilute your efforts and end up giving mediocre service to everyone. Decide which and how many of your customers you can realistically give remarkable service to.

Andy and Suzannah Coe founded Sussex Lighting in

2007, choosing to select high-quality premium-priced products for their showroom so they could attract their ideal customers. They have well trained and enthusiastic staff and they go out of their way to give remarkable service to their customers. If requested, they will visit their customers' homes to give advice and recommendations that suit each customer's tastes and needs.

However, they also know that as a specialist retailer, their resources are limited. It is simply not possible for them to offer remarkable service to everyone and so they carefully screen their customers before they make promises they can't keep, disregarding those who want something for nothing and concentrating on those who appreciate their expertise.

When you provide a remarkable service to your existing customers, asking for referrals and recommendations becomes easier and more natural. The best time to ask for a referral is at the moment you have given remarkable service because that's when your customer is enthusiastic and excited about your business. But you have to ask.

And yet most retailers and salespeople don't ask, either because they're so excited themselves about the sale and they forget, or they are scared. I have been in this situation myself many times, and when I have found the courage to ask, I have been pleasantly surprised every time.

Some common fears are that the customer will be offended and upset and they may even cancel the order. Other concerns are that you don't want to appear desperate or needy. After all, you run a successful business so why do you need to ask for referrals, right?

The truth is that if you want to catapult your business to the next level, you have to prospect, and this is the best and easiest place to start. What's the worst that can happen if you ask for referrals? The customer can say no, or they can say that they can't think of anyone. That's it. In my forty years of selling, I have never had anyone cancel a sale simply because I asked for referrals.

Notice I say referrals and not a referral. Always ask for more than one referral. If you ask your customer, 'Do you know anyone who might be interested in buying our products?', you are giving your customer the easy opt out to say no. A far more effective way to ask for referrals is to ask a question that can only be answered with a name, for example, 'I really appreciate your decision to buy from us and I would like to ask for your help. Who do you know who may also be interested in these products?' You can phrase the sentence to suit your needs, but the key words are 'Who do you know?' When you ask for referrals this way, you are helping your customer to think of specific people who may be in the market for your products. But you must remember to ask.

MARGINAL GAINS

In 2003, England won the Rugby World Cup, becoming the only nation from the Northern Hemisphere to have won the tournament. Most people who watched the game against Australia will put the victory down to one defining moment when Jonny Wilkinson landed a drop goal in the final minute of extra time to give England a 20–17 victory. I remember watching the game on TV with my family and our living room erupted into an explosion of joy and celebrations when he kicked the drop goal.

As nail biting and incredible as that drop goal was, the success of the England rugby team was not down to that. Instead, it was the result of a series of small improvements known as 'marginal gains' introduced by Sir Clive Woodward, who became England's first full-time coach in 1997. Woodward said that 'Winning the Rugby World Cup was not about doing one thing 100% better, but about doing 100 things 1% better'[3].

Before he became England coach, Woodward had been an entrepreneur who was meticulous about making small incremental gains that added up to a thriving and successful computer leasing company. He applied the same principles to the England rugby team by emphasising the importance of 'critical non-essentials' in the run up to the team's 2003 success. He allocated a room at the hotel to be the analysis room where the team could study the opposition to find anything that would give them even a small advantage. They had their own chef, visual awareness coach and kit technician, and Woodward brought in five-times Olympic gold medallist Sir Steve Redgrave as a motivational coach.

Now I appreciate that as an independent retailer, you probably don't have the budget to pay for these kind of assistants, but there are many marginal gains that you can implement that will cost little or no money. And prospecting is one of them.

So how can you apply the principle of marginal gains to your business? There are so many things that you can change or improve by 1% that it's impossible to list them all. But you are reading this book, so congratulations in taking the first step.

Let's have a look at a few more marginal gains from the world of prospecting.

OVERCOMING YOUR PROSPECTING GOLIATHS

There are three 'Goliaths' that prevent most of us from prospecting: procrastination, distractions and time. These same three elements can prevent us from making progress with the other four stones, too. If you can master these three Goliaths, you will be well equipped to implement everything taught in this book.

We will consider each of these Goliaths one at a time, but at the core of each is fear. The fear of rejection or the fear of failure.

Do you remember how you felt when you asked someone for a date for the first time? Or when you went for your first interview? Fear is a natural part of our DNA to help us avoid dangerous or hazardous situations. When we are confronted with danger, we have a choice: fight or flight. Depending on the situation, it may be wise to stand your ground and fight. At other times, it may make more sense to flee.

When it comes to prospecting, you need to make the conscious decision to fight your fears and the overwhelming desire to flee. The use of digital media is the least confrontational of your prospecting tools and is a vital part of your business, but to be truly effective you will need to make use of the phone and face-to-face prospecting. Then your results will improve significantly.

The biggest advantage of personal prospecting is that very few of your competitors use this approach. Think about it – when was the last time you received a phone call from your local retailer to tell you about a new range of products that had just arrived?

PROCRASTINATION

Imagine if a trusted friend walked into your business and enthusiastically presented you with the names of ten prospects who were waiting for your call. He had just spent the day with them at a networking event, and each one of them had told him that they were in the market for what you sell. He could even confirm that they would have the money to pay for your goods and services. What would be your response? Personally, I would stop what I was doing and phone each one of them there and then. I wouldn't hesitate because I wouldn't want to lose the sale.

So why do we procrastinate? I say 'we' because I fight this Goliath every day. And yet, when it comes to prospecting, I have overcome it more times than I can remember and have always been pleasantly surprised at the results.

The single biggest reason why people avoid prospecting is their fear of rejection, which is closely linked to their imagination. When it comes to confronting your fears, imagination weighs in on the side of procrastination and will feed your mind with a host of reasons not to take action: 'What if the customer shouts at me? What if they put the phone down? What if they tell people about me and I lose other customers? What will they think of me? I am a successful retailer, so why should I lower myself and beg for business? Besides, I'm busy running my shop and I don't have time for this.'

On and on it goes. And all the time your till is being robbed of flecks of gold because you keep putting off the need to prospect.

Moses was a prophet from the Old Testament who helped the Israelites escape from the Egyptians after many years of captivity. After their escape, he lead his people through the wilderness looking for a new home. According to the Bible, he sent twelve spies into the land of Canaan to gather intelligence to see if they could reclaim the land.

Ten of the spies reported that the people were strong and that the cities were surrounded by huge walls. They were scared to go into battle and so they exaggerated their story by saying that the enemy was far stronger than they really were, and that there were giants in the land. In fact, they claimed that the giants were so big that they, the spies, looked like grasshoppers in comparison.

But the other two spies, Joshua and Caleb, had a different perspective. They reminded their people that Canaan was a good land that was flowing with milk and honey. They told the people not to fear the enemy because the defences were weak and they could easily defeat them. Sadly, fear had already entered the hearts and minds of the people and they refused to go into battle. In fact, the Israelites were so fearful that they ended up wandering in the desert for forty years[4].

The consequences of listening to the voice of fear can be long lasting and sometimes devastating. No-one ever accomplished anything great by yielding to fear. Be of good courage and face your fear one step at a time.

When David faced Goliath, he knew he could win if he could pinpoint the giant's weakness. The one area that was exposed was Goliath's forehead and that's where David aimed his first stone. If he had focused his mind on the giant as a whole, he would have been paralysed by fear, just like his brothers.

When you face your fears, look for the opening. Look for the gap. There is always an opening if you act with courage. Focus on it. Don't be distracted by the voices of fear. After all, they are just voices, and you can change the message to suit your purpose. Make the voices of faith and courage your friends and they will lead you to positive action and success.

Here are three steps to help you overcome procrastination:

1. Replace fear with faith.
How do you do this? List all the reasons why you should make the prospecting call or ask for referrals. What will the benefits be when you prospect regularly? The more benefits you list, the more likely you will be to take action.

No amount of sophistication is going to allay the fact that all your knowledge is about the past and all your decisions are about the future.

Ian Wilson

Picture in your mind the perfect call. Imagine that you are prospecting and the person receiving your call is happy to hear from you. They are interested in what you are saying and they want to know more. You feel good about your chat and you invite them to your store or to visit your website, and they say yes.

Our minds are like movies. When we play the movie of rejection and fear, our minds will put obstacles in our way to avoid prospecting. However, if we repeatedly play the movie of a happy customer who is pleased to hear from us, our minds will find ways to help us make the call.

PREPARATION

The more prepared you are, the less you will fear and procrastinate. When you know what you are going to say and how you will handle any objections, you are in a stronger position to overcome your fears. In Stone Two we discussed how to create a compelling message. You may find it helpful to use all or part of this message in your prospecting approach. Practise with a friend or in front of the mirror before you make the call.

DISTRACTIONS

Distractions are closely linked to procrastination, but they are different in that you can control them with some preparation.

I am easily distracted. When I'm meant to be prospecting, I suddenly find myself checking my emails or have a desperate need to find out what's happening on social media. As I am writing this, a reminder has just popped up on my iPad that I promised to help a friend to lay some paving. How easy it would be to ring my friend and waste ten minutes chatting and setting a date. Of course, it's important that I follow through on my promise, but it's not a priority as she has told me it's not urgent.

When you are running a busy retail outlet, there are customers to serve, queries to solve, staff to manage, phone calls to make, tax returns to complete…the list goes on. These things are important, but there are other distractions that are less important – 'I need another cup of coffee'; 'Those displays need tidying up for the tenth time today' – yet we still allow them to get in the way of things like prospecting.

A distraction is something that prevents you from giving your full attention to whatever is important to you. If it's important for you to gain more ideal customers, then you need to give it your full attention. Begin by removing all the things that are likely to distract you. Ask your colleagues to answer the phone or serve customers while you are prospecting.

TIME

Not having enough time is the most common excuse for not prospecting, and it's one I have used myself.

I understand that you are probably living a crazily busy life and that there isn't time to do all the things you want to do, let alone the things you don't want to do. When it comes to prospecting, decide if it's a priority. It's that simple. Only when it becomes a priority in your business will you make the time for it consistently. And it's only when you recognise the value of prospecting, and the danger of what will happen if you don't prospect, that you will make it a priority.

There are many books about prospecting which cover all the things you need to do to become great at it. This section is intended to raise your awareness of the power of prospecting and hopefully inspire you to make it a central part of your marketing campaign. The lessons I have shared on prospecting are based on my personal experiences. For further reading, I would recommend my favourite book on the subject, which is *Fanatical Prospecting* by Jeb Blount. In this book, you will find pages of wonderful insights into the world of prospecting[5].

If you are in sales, you are always prospecting. In my early sales career, I would walk around the telephone many times before I plucked up the courage to make the call, breathing a huge sigh of relief if my prospect wasn't available to take it. Since then, I have walked the streets speaking to people about my products and I have climbed the stairs of tall office buildings, knocking on doors to find someone who would listen to my story. I have trembled with anxiety when asking for referrals, but it is fun and rewarding when I get it right.

For most salespeople, time-management problems are self-inflicted. The difference between highly successful retailers and those who are struggling is that top performers block out regular time for prospecting. They update their database and other resources before they begin prospecting so that they don't waste time thinking about whom to call. They also delegate non-essential activities to their staff or support team.

Prospecting is the lifeblood of any business, and there are so many effective ways to find new customers. When you master your time and maximise your prospecting efforts, sales will become a natural by-product.

SPEAKING ENGAGEMENTS

Perhaps one of the most powerful forms of prospecting for referrals is public speaking. When you make a presentation to a roomful of potential customers, you have a captive audience, and provided you have prepared your message, you have instant credibility.

I recently spoke at a conference in London, and without even trying, I received a handful of business cards from interested prospects. A businessperson could, if they wanted to, give two talks a day, seven days a week, at different venues. There are always opportunities to speak if you look for them.

A good place to start is to join your local chamber of commerce, or associations that are related to your industry. As an independent retailer, you need to speak where your customers are most likely to be found. You can offer to speak for free at a conference on a topic that is relevant to the audience.

When you ask to speak, assure the organisers that you won't try to sell the audience anything. Most organisations will not allow you to use their platform for sales. In exchange for your presentation, you can instead have an agreement to swap business cards with your audience, or you could offer them a free brochure about your business. Present content that is helpful, insightful or educational. Share your expertise freely; don't hold back.

The keys to a good speaking engagement are preparation and relevancy. If you are in fashion, speak about styling and how to dress well to make an impact. A furniture retailer could give advice on room settings and spatial awareness.

I appreciate that public speaking is a big fear for most people. In fact, it is the most common of all phobias, but like all fears, it can be overcome. There are hundreds of great books on public speaking and a host of courses you can attend. It's worth the effort to learn how to become a confident public speaker. The benefits of giving regular talks on your area of expertise are staggering, and most of your competitors won't be doing this.

PROACTIVE PROSPECTING

Getting in touch with buyers who are ready to buy from you is getting harder, especially with the rise of online marketing. Customers are well-informed and they have a wide range of choices across the country and from around the world.

However, the more familiar your customer is with your company, the more likely they will buy from you, or at least accept your call. People love to go back to their favourite restaurant or shop at familiar stores because they are comfortable and know what to expect. With a multi-pronged social media and advertising campaign, you can ensure your customers and prospects will become familiar with your company.

Prospecting can be tough, but if you make it a priority today, you will watch your business grow.

STONE FOUR SUMMARY

When you provide remarkable service to your existing customers, you are laying a foundation that will open doors to new customers. Word of mouth is a great way to get customers, but if you want to attract more ideal customers, you need to ask for referrals.

Prospecting is one way to make marginal gains. Marginal gains are not about doing one thing 100% better, they're about doing 100 things 1% better. Prospecting is hard, but when you replace your fears with faith in your abilities, you are better equipped to tackle the three Goliaths of procrastination, time and distractions.

1. M. Russell Ballard, 'Finding Joy through Loving Service'. General Conference of The Church of Jesus Christ of Latter-day Saints, April 2011

2. Priestley, D., *Oversubscribed: How to get people lining up to do business with you.* West Sussex, United Kingdom: Capstone, a Wiley brand, 2015, page 84.

3. Woodward, C., *Winning!* London: Hodder, 2005

4. Numbers 13–14, King James Version of the Bible.

5. Blount, J., *Fanatical Prospecting: The ultimate guide for starting sales conversations and filling the pipeline by leveraging social selling, telephone, email, and cold calling.* Hoboken, NJ: John Wiley & Sons, 2015

STONE FIVE

YOU ARE THE BRAND

Think about the Fortune 500 companies. How many can you name?

In the Top 100 are the likes of Walmart, Exxon Mobil, General Motors, General Electric, Costco, Amazon, Ford Motor, AT&T, IBM, Johnson and Johnson, FedEx and Coca Cola. In the UK, we have national chains such as John Lewis, House of Fraser and Debenhams.

Now think about how many CEOs you can name of these well known companies. I'm guessing relatively few. And here's where you can make a huge impact, because the biggest differentiator between you and the giants is you.

People buy from people, so the more customers know

about you in relation to your business, the greater the connection. Think about your local retailer. How well do you know them? Do you find yourself going back to the same shops because you have developed a strong relationship with the owner?

With the advent of social media, you now have the ability to develop a bond with your customers on a much bigger scale. As an independent retailer, you can leverage your unique personality to become the forefront of your business. By raising your personal profile, you create a special connection with your customer, even when you are not physically present.

When the Philistines prepared their armies for battle they gathered together in a place called Shochoh, while the men of Israel pitched their army by the Valley of Elah. The Philistines stood on one mountain and the Israelites watched on from another mountain on the opposite side of the valley[1].

Sometimes it feels like there is a valley between you and your customers, and trying to reach them is an impossible task. David didn't wait for Goliath to come to him in the valley of Elah. Instead, he made a plan and

ran towards Goliath. When you combine the power of
your personality with a well-planned social media strategy, you are literally running towards your customers.

Let's consider why it is so important to raise your personal profile. Imagine you are invited to pitch your business to the millionaire tycoons on the TV programme
Dragons Den. You spend months preparing your pitch
and you bring catalogues and product samples to show
them what you do.

With enthusiasm, you show the 'dragons' your products
and how well you've done since you started your business. You then demonstrate your fantastic website that il-
lustrates your products in beautiful colour with detailed
information. They are interested, but are not overly impressed. They ask you to take a seat while they interview
ten other retailers before they decide who to invest in.

You feel sure that you have impressed the dragons.
But as the other retailers make their presentations, you
begin to feel less confident. After the third or fourth
pitch, you see a pattern emerging.

When the presentations have finished, you come to the

sobering realisation that all ten companies are pretty much the same. The dragons can only invest in one retailer, and so they choose the one who offers them the biggest return on their investment.

As absurd as this example sounds, this is what hundreds of retailers do every day. They pitch products and services that are so similar to what's already out there that it is difficult for customers to differentiate. In addition to this, the big online retailers and nationals are doing the same thing, but on a grander and more spectacular scale. The customer then makes their purchase based on the best price.

Thankfully there is a cost-effective way to overcome this problem, and that is for you or a prominent member of your team to become the face of your business. When you become the face of the business, you add a personal dimension that cannot be replicated by any of your competitors. Your personality is unique, and when people get to know you, they will buy from you as they trust you. If people buy from you when they are in your showroom and like the personal service you give them and the attention to detail that you offer, you already have a measure of success with this. Now all you need to do is raise your profile so that your personality can be seen and heard on a grand scale.

Social media is a major key to getting your name and your personal profile to a wider audience. This, in addition to your existing website and speaking engagements, will help amplify your message.

When you add the ingredient of personality to your products and services, it's like adding sugar to your popcorn. Popcorn by itself is bland but edible. When you add a sweetener, it's delicious. Add your personality to your products and services, and your business becomes delicious, too.

We will discuss the mechanics of social media later on in this section, but for now let's look at why adding a dash of personality to your business is so powerful.

A DASH OF PERSONALITY

When you add a dash of personality, everything changes. Customers don't just see you as a commodity, they see you as a real person and they are able to make an emotional connection.

Jamie Oliver is a well known TV chef who makes great recipes, but people tune in to watch his shows because they enjoy his vibrant and fun personality. Mary Berry is the nation's favourite baking grandma and we love to sit at her feet and listen to her wise words of advice.

Jamie and Mary are both cooks, and you could argue that they do pretty much the same thing. And yet they have carved their own unique niche in the marketplace. If cookery programmes were just about cooking and baking, TV producers would save a fortune in celebrity chefs and just get someone to narrate the recipes from the sidelines. But that would be bland and boring.

When you add a dash of personality to your business, you become a celebrity. You don't need to become a national celebrity, just a celebrity within your local industry.

By sharing your unique insights and expertise with your customers, you will transform your business from a faceless retailer to a vibrant personality. When you are the brand, you draw customers to your products and services and they listen to your message. If you choose not to develop your own personal brand, others will do it for you and you may not like the results. When you are proactive in developing your personal brand, you control how you are perceived in the marketplace.

There are five things you will need to consider when developing your personal brand.

1. Personalise your website.
Your website should include your personal brand and feature you as part of your products and services. This is where customers will become familiar with who you are and what you represent, but be careful not to overshadow your products. You are there to enhance your products and services, not replace them.

Your website is a great place to post regular blogs where you can share your insights and expertise. When you share your content on social media and other platforms, remember to add your own personality to the mix. Share personal stories that will create an emotional connection with your audience. Unless you are an inventor or innovator, you will have nothing new to add to your field of expertise. However, your unique personality and your style will help your customers see your solutions in a different light.

2. Identify what makes you unique.
In Stone Two we made a list of the reasons our customers should buy from us. This time, consider what it is about you and your personality that makes you unique. How are your talents and gifts an asset to your business? How will they benefit your customers?

This can get a little uncomfortable because no-one likes to boast about themselves. But this is not about showing off; it's about discovering what you are good at. What makes you different? What makes you unique? What skills do you have that relate to your industry?

Make a list of your unique strengths and talents in the context of how they can help and benefit your customers. When you make an inventory with your customers' best interests in mind, it is less self-serving. If you are struggling to make a list, ask a trusted friend or a family member to help you.

On your list of strengths, which ones are currently under-appreciated by your customers? Sometimes you have a strength that you and your staff are aware of, but most of your customers don't recognise, or if they do, they don't fully appreciate that it is unique to you. How can you make your customers aware of your skills and talents in a way that will benefit them and persuade them to buy from you?

3. What do you want to be known for?

What is your emotional appeal? Why do people like you? Take a few moments to consider why you think people are drawn to your personal brand. What do you want to be known for?

Our local butcher is a master butcher and is often featured in newspapers and radio interviews for winning numerous awards. He is well known for his sense of humour and his obsession for cleanliness (which is good to know if you want to buy meat from him).

4. Become the expert.

Once you have identified your unique strengths, perfect and build on them. As a specialist retailer, you need to become the expert in your field. This is what will separate you from your competition and will draw more customers to your store.

You may be feeling a little inadequate right now and that's OK. Being an expert in your field requires a lifetime of discovery and learning, but my hunch is you already know enough to get started.

5. Share your knowledge and expertise.
You have a wealth of knowledge and experience which is not much use to you unless you share it. Share it freely with the intention of enriching and helping others. In social media marketing, content is key to your business success, not products.

Building your personal brand will take time and effort, but it will be worth it. Digital media will continue to increase and the need for you to become a personal brand will continue to grow. The great thing about having a strong personal brand is that it's transferable, an asset that you can take with you whatever your business.

Your personal brand evolves over time, and with experience you will develop different skills and talents. Customers don't always know about your experience or how your expertise relates to them. What are your customers' unrecognised needs? How do you get them to think differently about you?

The best way to get your customers to think differently about you is to get them to think differently about themselves. What are your customers thinking? What are they missing? Remember, the goal isn't so much to convince them to buy a solution, but rather to persuade them to change their behaviour.

I remember an excellent advertising campaign in South Africa in the 1990s for car wiper blades. Most people associate the deterioration of wiper blades with excessive use in rainy weather. But the weather in South Africa is bright and sunny for most of the year. You would think that people would need to change their wiper blades less often than drivers in the rainy UK, for instance.

However, this company did its homework and discovered that harsh weather conditions reduced the life of car wiper blades, even when it wasn't raining. Normal use, sunlight and dust was causing the rubber on the blades to dry out and crack. These defects caused streaking on the windscreen and reduced visibility in wet weather.

Almost overnight, the company changed the buying behaviour of many South African drivers. Instead of just changing their wiper blades in wet weather, customers were buying new wiper blades in the middle of summer.

How can you change your customers' buying behaviour? How can you help them to see your products and services differently?

When you understand the real problems of your customer, you are in a better position to define your brand and your purpose and focus on your unique strengths.

We thought we were selling the transportation of goods, when in fact we were selling peace of mind.

Frederick W. Smith, Chair and CEO of FedEx[2]

With this mindset, FedEx was able to take the frustration out of transporting goods, allowing its customers to rest assured that their goods would arrive on time and in one piece.

When you build your personal brand with your customers' unrecognised needs in mind, you will create a brand tailored around their wishes and desires rather than you as a retailer.

SOCIAL MEDIA AND PERSONAL BRANDING

When you have defined your brand and you understand your customers' needs, you are in a strong position to use social media to get yourself noticed. The key is to provide helpful and insightful content, and to do this repeatedly. We will discuss this more in 'Content is key'.

There are numerous social media platforms that you can use, and I recognise that there are new companies entering the market all the time. For this reason, I will mention just a few well known social media websites and how they can be of benefit. But for now, let's have a look at what drives social media.

Social media is just social networking but on the internet. People have been social networking for centuries, from rural market towns in medieval times to Starbucks today. At various social venues, people would relax with their friends and family and talk about anything and everything, sharing ideas, advice or recipes. And yes, they would also show photographs from their latest holiday (well, perhaps not in medieval times...)

Does this sound familiar? Social media is just an extension of our social network on a worldwide platform. People mainly go on to social media to be with their friends and find new ones. They want to share ideas and learn new things, and occasionally they may buy something. But the primary purpose of social media is not to sell your products and services.

I remember chatting with some friends at a social gathering. They told me they were moving home and needed new lights. Knowing that I was in the lighting business, they asked me to drop a catalogue off the next day. I didn't try and sell them anything at the social event, but I was able to offer them some tips and advice which led to a sale.

Listening and sharing ideas will bring you success on social media. Before you can attract a following of loyal customers, you need to engage in conversation with them and gain their trust. As you share useful content on social media, potential buyers will become interested in what you have to say, which will lead them to your website or store. By offering genuinely helpful insights, you will generate followers who will eventually become customers.

People buy from people they trust and have a connection with. How do you build a relationship of trust to the point where your customer considers you a friend who has their best interests at heart?

It takes time. Think about the closest friend you have. In the beginning, you noticed you had some things in common. Perhaps you went to the movies together, played the same games or socialised with each other. Without any conscious effort, you nourished your friendship with small acts of kindness, which were reciprocated by your friend. Over time, you learned to trust each other, and now you can depend on each other in good and bad times.

Social media is an ideal place to build a connection and earn your customers' trust. You can create ongoing connections with your audience even when you are not present as social media platforms provide you with opportunities to share how-to videos, DIY tips, podcasts and great content.

There are so many amazing social media platforms you can use, but here are a few examples of the more popular ones.

BLOGS

Blogs are a great place to start because you can quickly and easily write meaningful content with pictures. They can be mounted on your website, and people who visit your website can leave comments and feedback.

Blogs can be a powerful source of search engine traffic, but make sure that your blog is linked to your website where most business takes place. Publishing regular blog posts with insightful and helpful content is a powerful way to grow your business.

Having a blog with useful and up to the minute content will help strengthen your relationship with your core customers. When you freely share your expertise in this medium, trust levels increase and your customers will appreciate your openness and transparency. If you choose to invite feedback, check in regularly so that you can respond.

It is important to blog regularly, and I would recommend at least once a week to keep your customers' interest. It's worth the effort because the content that you write can easily be transposed to podcasts, Facebook, YouTube videos and various other social media websites.

Podcasts

Podcasting is like a blog but in audio. People are on the move these days and they often listen to articles of interest while they are travelling. I recently missed a training course, but I was grateful to be able to catch up via a podcast while I was driving. Starting and maintaining a podcast is a little more complicated than a blog, but with a decent microphone and a simple editing app, you can get great results.

Twitter

Twitter is a popular medium for celebrities, politicians and top businesses as it provides its followers with instant updates. Be careful, though, as Twitter is available for the whole world to see, so make sure that you double check what you post.

The main advantages of Twitter are that it's the fastest way to grow a targeted audience and it offers a variety of advertising platforms. Current research shows that customers who follow you on Twitter tend to be very loyal.

Facebook

Facebook is the largest social media website in the world today, and is considered a key part of daily life for many people. This global phenomenon is unsurpassed in its ability to connect businesses with customers in a friendly and relaxed way. It is an ideal way to get your message out quickly and monitor the reactions of your potential and existing customers.

You can either use a personal Facebook page or create a business page. If you want to keep information about your family and friends private, you may want to open a business page early on.

The advantages of Facebook for business are that it's easy to target the demographics of your industry and you can tailor your message for a customised audience. You can also boost posts so that they are seen in newsfeeds more frequently to generate more interactions.

Starting a basic Facebook page for your business is free and you can post content that includes links to your website, products, or blogs. Every business has brand ambassadors who love it and are happy to share positive experiences with their family and friends. Facebook makes it easier than ever for them to share these experiences with friends all over the world.

Measuring your results is easy, too. You will be able to see how many people are 'liking' your page, how many are seeing your page, and how many clicks and shares you are generating. By measuring this data on a daily or weekly basis, you can discover what content is popular and what content is not.

LINKEDIN

LinkedIn is known as the social network for professionals and businesses. It acts like an online CV, detailing your education, business skill, experiences and recommendations from your colleagues and friends. It can be used to post blogs and advertise your business portfolio, but it is mainly used for business to business connections and sales. It is a great place to learn, gain insights and to get feedback from others in your profession.

LinkedIn works well for small businesses as it can improve your search engine optimisation (SEO), especially when you have excellent content. SEO affects the visibility of your website. The more frequently people visit your website, the higher ranked you'll become, which increases your chances of appearing on the front page of Google or other search engines.

You can create content for LinkedIn which can be shared as an article link to other social media sites like Facebook or Twitter. This means that the main parts of your content will have increased exposure and can lead to better overall conversion rates. With LinkedIn for business, you are able to tap into your niche market without the need to develop your own site, and it's a fast way to establish personal credibility in your industry.

YOUTUBE

Youtube. Billions of videos are viewed on YouTube every day. Although this may seem daunting, there is still space for small businesses to get noticed.

It's worth investing time and money to create good quality videos for this medium. YouTube is owned by Google, which means that your rating will increase on its search engine and lead more people to your website. The first place that people go to find your products or services is an internet search engine, then a social media platform and then your website. And yet most retailers have this back to front. They invest most of their time and money in their website, then on social media and then on search engines.

By posting regular content on some or all of the social media platforms discussed here, you will find your name and brand will feature more often on the front page of Google.

CONTENT IS KEY

If the social web were a living organism, content would be the air that it breathes.

Mark W. Schaefer[3]

There is no shortage of information and most of it can be found free on the internet. And yet your ability to create and publish original content on the web that gets shared throughout the world is limitless. But how can you create original content when there is already so much information about your products and services? Because you have experiences and insights that are unique to you.

Have you ever watched a celebrity or an expert being interviewed on TV or social media? If they are someone you admire and respect, you will listen with interest and often find their responses and stories compelling and engaging. Yet if you analysed what they were saying, most of the time it's nothing new. You continue to watch or listen because you have become emotionally connected.

The same applies when you share information and insights about your business and products. Your followers may sense that some of your content is familiar, but you are giving it from your unique perspective. It's personal to you, and people love to engage with those who are authentic and real. They are especially interested in people who care about their problems.

When we are in a social situation, the people we tend to avoid are the ones who drone on endlessly about themselves. The people who inspire us are the ones who show a genuine interest in us and our problems. This principle of caring for others is no different on social media. When your followers know that you really care, they will remain engaged and listen to what you have to say.

During elections, it's fascinating to watch politicians responding to questions from interviewers. No matter their political allegiance, they all seem to have a need to step on their soap box and list all the reasons why the viewers should vote for them. Nobody likes to be shouted at, but we will listen to people whom we believe in and who really care.

Step away from your soap box and speak or write from your heart.

WHEN AND HOW TO SELL ON SOCIAL MEDIA

We are in business to sell products and services. While we need to share great content, provide insights and give tips, at some point we need customers to buy our products. While we don't want to be like a politician on a soap box, we do need to give our prospective customers plenty of opportunities to buy from us.

Make it easy for them to buy from you by implementing the call to action incentives discussed in Stone Two – How To Create A Compelling Message.

MEASURING RESULTS

Measuring results on social media is easier than you think as there is a lot of data available for digital marketing. You could use a free programme like Google Analytics that provides a rich source of information about who is visiting your site, what content is working for you, and countless other insights.

Not all of the statistics you receive will give you a financial measurement, but you will be able to measure the quality of your investment. Being invited to speak at a conference, having your blog content posted on an influential website, or having an article written about you are all great returns on your investment, even though they are not easy to measure financially.

What kind of behaviours and attitudes are you trying to influence through your social media marketing? In a year from now, what would a successful social media campaign look like? Once you know this, it is easier to find the appropriate measurements that relate to your goals.

There are many ways to measure the return on your investment (ROI) from social media and I strongly recommend that you create a spreadsheet that works for you. I know spreadsheets can be boring, but they can also be very rewarding when you see the results of your hard work. However you choose to measure your social media marketing, you must measure it, otherwise how will you know if you are getting a return on your investment?

I have spoken to numerous retailers about the power of social media and how they can use it to attract more of the right kind of customers, and I am occasionally met with a negative response. I recall one retailer telling me that they had over six thousand followers on Facebook but they had hardly made any sales. When I viewed their Facebook page, I could see that they had made the classic social media mistake of peddling their products on a massive scale. This either turns customers off or drives them to price match and buy the same products elsewhere.

Sadly, this once thriving retailer went out of business recently.

Social media for business is about generating content and leads that result in sales, not the other way around.

STONE FIVE SUMMARY

Big business is often faceless and impersonal. The biggest differentiator between you and the giants is you.

When you become the face of your business, you add a personal dimension that cannot be replicated by your competitors. By sharing your unique insights and expertise on social media, you will make your business known to a worldwide audience.

The key to getting noticed is posting regular content for your target customer. You can post useful content on Facebook, LinkedIn, YouTube or other social media platforms once a week, monthly or even daily. Remember to measure your results so you know what your ROI is and how you can improve. This can be done by downloading a free programme such as Google Analytics, or you could use a simple spreadsheet.

1. Samuel 17:1–3, King James Version of the Bible.
2. Wyborny, S., *Frederick W. Smith: Founder of FedEx*. Detroit: GreenHaven Press, 2008.
3. Schaefer, M. W., *Social Media Explained: Untangling the world's most misunderstood business trend*. S.l.: S.n., 2014.

Conclusion

Begin by knowing that you have already arrived.

Richard Bach

As I write the conclusion of my book, I am sitting in a holiday cottage overlooking the beautiful Brixham Harbour in Devon. It's a wonderful summer's day and seagulls are soaring over the bay. As I watch them scavenging for food from the trawlers, I am reminded of an inspiring book I read in the 1970s called *Jonathan Livingston Seagull* by Richard Bach[1].

The book tells the story of a seagull called Jonathan Livingston Seagull who has a passion for flying and pushes himself to learn everything he can about it. He becomes unwilling to conform to the daily grind of hunting for food until he is eventually expelled from the seagull colony.

As an outcast, he continues to learn about flight and becomes increasingly pleased with his abilities to fly at great heights and speed. One day, Jonathan meets two other gulls who take him to a 'higher plane of existence' where there is a better world to be found through the perfection of knowledge. He discovers that through sheer tenacity and his desire to learn that he was 'pretty well a one-in-a-million bird'.

In this book, I have spoken about your unique personality and how you can make a significant difference in your field of expertise. It is my genuine belief that you are 'pretty well a one-in-a-million' retailer. I do not say this lightly, because I have met many great retailers who meet this criterion.

Your business can soar to a 'higher plane of existence' through learning and application, but only if you take courage like David and face your Goliaths with determination and zeal.

Having courage is not a one-off event. Courage needs

to be cultivated and used regularly. David had already faced perilous situations before he conquered Goliath when he defended his father's sheep from the lion and the bear. For his part, Goliath taunted the Israelite army every day for forty days. He was relentless.

As an independent retailer, you will be challenged with problems every day. Like Goliath, they are relentless. At some point, you have to face the reality of your situation and do whatever it takes to make the changes you need to soar to a higher plane.

David only needed one stone to defeat Goliath, but I have given you five stones to help you take on your giants. One of the greatest fears is the fear of the unknown, but with these five stones you have the knowledge you need to overcome your Goliaths.

When you know who your ideal customer is and you have a compelling message, it is easier to have courage to take on the giants in your industry. With the right products and a well organised prospecting method in place, you can grow your faith in your ability to succeed exponentially. Add to this an effective personal branding campaign and you become unstoppable.

What I've written in this book is less important than what you have learned or felt. There is another dynamic that comes into play whenever you read a 'how to' or inspirational book, and that is the dynamic of intuition. As you have been reading, there's a chance your mind will have inspired you with ideas and impressions about your business. You may have considered ways to improve and change your business and made notes of the things that you want to implement.

In the end, it's the implementation of the ideas in this book that will make the difference. Good luck with transforming your business from an independent retailer to a specialist retailer; I would love to hear your story.

There will always be a need for independent retailers, but it's the specialist retailer that will rise above the average every time. Let's make this great country a nation of specialist retailers. And it begins with one retailer at a time.

Why not take your first step today?

1. Bach, R. and Munson, R. *Jonathan Livingston Seagull:* A story. London: Harper Thorsons, 2015

Acknowledgements

Writing this book has been exhilarating and stretching in ways I didn't think were possible. Thankfully, I didn't have to write it on my own and I am so grateful for friends and family who helped me to stay focused and inspired with words and messages of encouragement.

I would like to thank Lucy McCarraher and her team for their patience and professional insight as they guided me through the exciting world of book writing. I am also deeply grateful to my good friend Elaine Gilboy who read and re-read many manuscripts and who had the courage to give me direct advice and helpful suggestions when needed.

A special thank you to the KPI community at Dent Global who acted as a sounding board. I shared many ideas and thoughts with them and they always responded in a positive and constructive way. Thank you to Ian Dormer and Andy Coe who were brave enough to read the very first draft and who gave me some amazing and helpful feedback.

Thank you to my wonderful family who have inspired and encouraged me to keep on writing. My greatest supporter is my wife who allowed me to spend many hours in my office writing without complaining. Thank you, Carla.

Thank you to the many independent retailers who helped me with the research that lead to the formulation of the five steps outlined in my book. A big thank you to all the courageous independent retailers who take on the giants every day and who bring a personal touch to our local communities.

Lastly, I would like to thank my late father Derek Retallick who lived and breathed retail and who inspired me to follow my dreams.

Author

Ian Retallick has been supplying decorative lighting to independent retailers and department stores for nearly twenty years and has learnt from first-hand experience the challenge independent retailers face in running a profitable business. Ian has over forty years of sales and business experience and has built a successful business with a reputation for putting the customer before the sale.

He has learnt and applied the five stones of selling (outlined in this book) in his own life and invites you to discover how applying them can positively transform your retail business. Ian comes from a family of retailers and worked with his father who was in retail his whole life. As a small boy he would watch his dad skilfully and patiently help customers to find that special something that was personal to them.

Ian's early career was not all roses and in his first twenty years of business he had twelve jobs and four business failures. However, he believes that life is a great teacher and he learnt some valuable lessons from these setbacks. In 2007, he started his fifth business as an independent supplier of lighting and has built a successful agency winning Agent of the Year from the MAA (Manufacturer's Agents Association) in 2017.

The High Street has undergone a seismic shock since the rise of the internet giants but Ian believes that customers still want personal service that can only be provided by the independent retailer. The old rules of selling for bricks-and-mortar retailers no longer apply and a new way of thinking is urgently required. After many years of research and study, Ian has formulated a five-step plan that is relevant to today's fast moving global market. These ideas have been tested and proven in other markets and he invites you to apply them to your business.

WHAT NEXT?

Ian Retallick is an accomplished speaker and is well known for helping retailers to crystallise their thinking. Why not invite Ian to your next event and discover how specialist retailers consistently outperform independent retailers.

He also writes a weekly blog where he shares inspirational ideas to help independent retailers to stay ahead of the giants and grow their business.

You can find more information on
www.ianretallick.com